Jonathan P. Tomes, J.D.

Antitrust Law

Other Books in the Guide for the Healthcare Professional Series

Environmental Law, by Jonathan P. Tomes, 1993

Fraud, Waste, Abuse and Safe Harbors, by Jonathan P. Tomes, 1993

Healthcare EDI, by James J. Moynihan, 1993

Industry Regulation, by Jonathan P. Tomes, 1993

Jonathan P. Tomes, J.D.

Antitrust Law

A Guide for the Healthcare Professional

PROBUS PUBLISHING COMPANY
Chicago, Illinois
Cambridge, England

 HEALTHCARE FINANCIAL MANAGEMENT ASSOCIATION

HFMA gratefully acknowledges the gracious assistance of the following content reviewers for this book: Allan P. DeKaye, CMPA; Terry E. Erwine, FHFMA; Robert E. Fisher, FHFMA; Joan C. Hoffman, FHFMA; R. R. Kovener, FHFMA; and Arnold R. Saitow, FHFMA.

Copyright © 1993 by Healthcare Financial Management Association
FIRST EDITION
FIRST PRINTING—1993

All rights reserved. No part of this publication may be reproduced, stored in a retrieval system, or transmitted, in any form or by any means, electronic, mechanical, photocopying, recording, or otherwise, without the prior written permission of the copyright owner.

Although every precaution has been taken in the preparation of this book, the publisher and author assume no responsibility for errors or omissions. Neither is any liability assumed for damages resulting from the use of the information contained herein.

Printed in the United States of America

Library of Congress Cataloging-in-Publication Data

Tomes, Jonathan P.
    The healthcare financial manager's guide to antitrust law issues / by Jonathan P. Tomes.
      p. cm.
    Includes bibliographical references and index.
    ISBN 1-882198-02-6 $37.95
    1. Health facilities—Law and legislation—United States.
2. Medical care—Law and legislation—United States. 3. Antitrust law—United States. 4. Health facilities—United States—Business management.
I. Title.
KF3825.T64 1993
344.73'0721—dc20
[347.303721]
                                                92-35486
                                                  CIP

10 9 8 7 6 5 4 3 2 1

Contents

Chapter 1: The Healthcare Antitrust Problem, 1

Chapter 2: An Overview of Antitrust Law, 5
History and Background of Antitrust Law, 5
United States Congressional Acts Concerning Antitrust Issues, 7
State Antitrust Statutes, 11

Chapter 3: Antitrust Law and the Healthcare Industry, 13
Does Antitrust Law Apply to Healthcare Professionals? 13
Application of the Antitrust Laws to Businesses and Professions, 14
The Nonprofit Exemption, 15
The Governmental Exemption, 16
The Insurance Exemption, 17
Peer Review Immunity, 19
Preemption by Other Laws, 19

Chapter 4: Antitrust Problems in Mergers, Acquisitions, and Affiliations, 21

Increased Antitrust Scrutiny of Mergers, 22
Antitrust Laws Governing Mergers, 23
Reporting Requirements, 25
Analyzing a Merger for Antitrust Problems, 26
Decreasing the Risk of an Antitrust Violation, 33

Chapter 5: Antitrust and Other Arrangements Among Healthcare Providers, 35

Background, 36
How Can a Professional Association Violate Antitrust Laws?, 36
HMOs, PPOs, and the Antitrust Laws, 38
Price Fixing, 38
Most-Favored-Nation Clauses, 41
Boycotts by Healthcare Providers, 42
Exclusive Dealing by Healthcare Providers, 43
Exclusive Contracting With Physicians, 43
Conversions from Not-for-Profit to For-Profit Status, 44

Chapter 6: Antitrust and Access to Facilities and Organizations, 47

History of Regulating the Practice of the Healing Arts, 48
The Requirement for Staff Privileges and Peer Review, 48
Antitrust Implications of Staff Privileges and Peer Review, 50
The Health Care Quality Improvement Act, 52
Economic Credentialing, 56

Chapter 7: Antitrust Aspects of Pricing Healthcare Goods and Services, 59

The Robinson-Patman Act, 59

Chapter 8: Sanctions for Antitrust Violations, 63
Criminal Sanctions for Violation of the Antitrust Laws, 63
Awards and Penalties in Civil Suits, 64

Glossary, 67

Bibliography, 71

Index, 75

About the Author, 81

The Healthcare Antitrust Problem

A review of healthcare publications in the past two years reveals the existence of a significant problem for healthcare providers in the area of antitrust law. The following are just a few article titles on this subject

- ❖ "Court Refuses to Dismiss Action Alleging Hospital's Pyramid Residency Program Violates Sherman Act"
- ❖ "Antitrust: Evidence of Bad Faith During Peer Review Creates Inference of Conspiracy in Restraint of Trade"
- ❖ "Public Hospital Not Immune from Liability for Anticompetitive Activity"
- ❖ "Mixed Signals from Government Have Chilling Effect on Mergers"
- ❖ "Utah University Hospital Pulls Out of Heart Transplant Cooperative"

An article in *Hospitals 1990*[1] noted that hospitals are using consultants for legal problems more than for any other purpose; 61 percent of hospitals planned to do so in 1990. The survey listed

---

1. Howard Anderson, "Legal and Strategic Consulting Most in Demand," *Hospitals 1990* 64, No. 13 (July 5, 1990), pp. 22-27.

antitrust as one of the most pressing legal problems of healthcare facilities. In another article, 3,400 CEOs were surveyed. Fifty-eight percent had revised the fair hearing and appellate review provisions in their bylaws governing medical staff reappointments to try to prevent antitrust suits.[2]

Even more recently, two federal courts addressed healthcare antitrust law. In the late spring of 1991, the United States Court of Appeals for the Ninth Circuit ruled that a public hospital is not immune from liability for anticompetitive activity and the Fourth Circuit held that the Sherman Antitrust Act applied to hospital peer review decisions.[3]

One healthcare law expert has noted that the federal government currently has "intense interest in healthcare antitrust in comparison to much lesser interest in most of the rest of the United States' economy."[4]

Further, with declining hospital occupancy and revenues and with the trend toward elimination of excess bed capacity, healthcare providers are considering alternatives such as mergers and affiliations with other healthcare providers to increase operating efficiency and reduce costs. These arrangements have important antitrust considerations, and the federal government has responded by increasing its scrutiny.[5]

As a financial manager, you obviously need to manage your assets so that the facility can provide needed services at the most efficient level in today's healthcare environment.[6] A financial manager cannot enter into a service contract with another healthcare provider without considering whether doing so violates antitrust law. Similarly, before your facility considers acquiring another healthcare facility, merging with another organization, affiliating

---

2. Mary Koska, "Medical Staff Changes Reflect External Pressure," *Hospitals 1990* 64, No. 22 (November 20, 1990), p. 54.
3. "Casenotes: Antitrust: Public Hospital Not Immune from Liability for Anticompetitive Activity," *Hospital Law* 24, No. 6 (June 1991), p. 193; "Casenotes: Antitrust: Intracorporate Immunity Does Not Shield Peer Review from Sherman Act Claims," *Hospital Law* 24, No. 5 (May 1991), p. 148.
4. Harold Bressler, "Antitrust Issues in the Healthcare Field: An Introduction," *Hospital Law* 32, No. 4 (April 1990), p. 101.
5. *See, generally,* Anne Murphy, "Application of Federal Antitrust Laws to Hospital Mergers: Understand the Evolving Rules," *Hospital Law* 32, No. 4 (April 1990), p. 101.
6. Russell Caruana, *Organizing a Healthcare Financial Services Division,* 3d ed. (Westchester, Ill.: Healthcare Financial Management Association, 1990), p. 5.

with another organization, or revising your procedures for removing staff privileges, it must consider the antitrust aspects of doing so. The remainder of this book will help you understand this most critical area of healthcare law so that you and your fellow key officers are able to ensure that your facility is responsive to the changing healthcare environment without running afoul of the antitrust laws.

At the minimum, financial managers should be aware of the potential for antitrust violations in many common healthcare business arrangements in order to know when to consult with legal counsel. To help you do this, chapter 2 provides you with an overview of antitrust law in general and chapter 3 discusses whether it may apply to your healthcare organization. The remainder of the book discusses particular antitrust problems healthcare providers face. Antitrust problems in mergers, acquisitions, and affiliations are discussed in chapter 4, and chapter 5 covers how antitrust law relates to professional and other associations. Chapter 6 surveys another critical area in antitrust law, that of granting or denying provider access to facilities and services. Chapter 7 discusses the pricing of health services, especially with regards to health insurers, health maintenance organizations, and preferred provider organizations. Finally, chapter 8 explains the possible sanctions for violations of the antitrust laws.

An Overview of Antitrust Law

In order for you, as a healthcare financial manager, to understand healthcare antitrust law, you should have a basic familiarity with antitrust law in general. A history of antitrust law can provide you with an understanding of these key acts and statutes: the Sherman Act, the Clayton Act, the Federal Trade Commission Act, and state antitrust statutes.

❖ History and Background of Antitrust Law

Broadly speaking, antitrust laws are statutes that the government enacted to promote free competition in the marketplace. As early as the sixteenth century, the English courts began to oppose the monopolistic arrangements such as guilds granted by charter from the crown. However, this regulatory trend did not become prominent until the end of the sixteenth century when it was exported to the colonies. The Americans felt strongly that monopolies ran counter to the individualistic character of liberty that came to be embodied in the Declaration of Independence.

Thus, the American common law against monopolies became a tradition that led to the enactment of the antitrust laws, the most important of which was the Sherman Antitrust Act in 1890. Congress passed this act as a response to the large national trusts of the time, such as the Standard Oil Trust and the American Cotton Trust. In these and similar trusts, competitors formed combinations to set prices and divide markets, thus creating monopolies and driving up prices. Among the goals of the Sherman Act was to protect consumers by promoting full and free competition. Such competition benefited the consumer by creating a market of lower-priced, higher-quality goods and services.[1]

In addition, many states enacted similar antitrust statutes. And anticompetitive practices by railroads, such as price fixing, led to the enactment of the Interstate Commerce Act to regulate them. This act established the Interstate Commerce Commission and granted it the authority to regulate the interstate rates charged by railroads to ensure they would be reasonable.[2]

As businesses became more varied and complex, the federal and state governments broadened the scope of the antitrust laws to cover more and more business activities.

Not only do individual consumers benefit from these laws, business consumers benefit as well. Your facility would have to pay a lot more for disposable hypodermic needles or medical waste disposal services if the seller of the product or service had a monopoly and could set the price as high as it wished without fear of competition. And with the high cost of health care and the small operating margins of healthcare providers, neither providers nor their patients can afford artificially high prices for products and services necessary to operate the facility and provide the care. As the United States Supreme Court stressed:

> Antitrust laws in general, and the Sherman Act in particular, are the Magna Carta of free enterprise. They are as important to the preservation of economic freedom and our free-enterprise system as the Bill of Rights is to the protection of our personal freedoms. And the freedom guaranteed each and every business, no matter how small, is the freedom to compete—to assert with vigor, imagination, devotion, and ingenuity whatever economic muscle it can muster.[3]

---

1. William Letwin, *Law and Economic Policy in America* (1965), pp. 18-32.
2. Ch. 104, 24 Stat. 379 (1887) (codified as amended at 49 U.S.C. §§ 10101-11917 (Supp. IV 1980).
3. United States v. Topco Associates Inc., 405 U.S. 596, 610 (1972).

❖ United States Congressional Acts Concerning Antitrust Issues

Three federal laws, the Sherman Act, the Clayton Act, and the Federal Trade Commission Act regulate federal antitrust issues.

The Sherman Act

The 1890 Sherman Act, with only minor amendments, remains in force today.[4] It has two basic sections that differ primarily because Section 1 requires an agreement—concerted action between two or more individuals or entities—and has a broader scope than Section 2, which does not require an agreement and applies only to monopolies. Section 1 states that:

> Every contract, combination in the form of trust or otherwise, or conspiracy in restraint of trade or commerce among the several States, or with foreign nations, is hereby declared to be illegal. Every person who shall make any contract or engage in any combination or conspiracy hereby declared to be illegal shall be deemed guilty of a felony and, on conviction thereof, shall be punished by fine not exceeding one million dollars if a corporation, or, if any other person, one hundred thousand dollars, or by imprisonment not exceeding three years, or by both said punishments, in the discretion of the court.

Section 1 is very broad. Congress did not limit it to particular types of businesses. It does not distinguish between businesses that provide products and those that offer services. However, because it only applies to contracts, combinations, and conspiracies, it must involve more than one individual or entity.[5] Although its language is broad, the courts have interpreted Section 1 as prohibiting only unreasonable restraints of trade.[6] The United States Supreme Court formulated the so-called rule-of-reason test:

---

4. 15 U.S.C. § 1 (1988).
5. Martin V. Thompson, *Antitrust and the Healthcare Provider* (Germantown, Md.: Aspen Systems Corp., 1979), p. 3 (hereinafter, Thompson).
6. *Id. See also* Edward Matto, *A Manager's Guide to the Antitrust Laws* (New York: AMACOM, 1980), p. 7 (hereinafter, Matto).

> The true test of legality is whether the restraint imposed is such as merely regulates and perhaps thereby promotes competition or whether it is such as may suppress or even destroy competition. To determine that question the court must ordinarily consider the facts peculiar to the business to which the restraint was imposed; the nature of the restraint and its effect, actual or probable. The history of the restraint, the evil believed to exist, the reason for adopting the particular remedy, the purpose or end sought to be attained are all relevant facts.[7]

Perhaps because the inquiry into whether a particular transaction passes the rule-of-reason test is very complicated, the courts have also developed a second category apart from the rule-of-reason category: the per se rule. Under this rule, some agreements are always illegal regardless of the circumstances, and the court does not have to look at the factors explained earlier.

Per se violations include price fixing, division of markets, group boycotts, and tying arrangements. *Price fixing* is nothing more than an agreement among competitors establishing a common price for their products. An example in the healthcare industry would be an agreement between physicians to all charge the same amount for a particular treatment or even to merely follow a medical association suggested fee schedule. For example, in 1990, the Justice Department filed the first criminal antitrust case against a healthcare provider in 50 years when it charged three dentists with conspiring (concerted action) to fix prices for dental services covered by prepaid dental plans.[8] (See chapter 7 on the pricing of health services.)

Division of markets involves two or more competitors agreeing to split up the market, such as two or more healthcare facilities in a certain geographic area agreeing to split up the patients according to where they live.

A *group boycott* is an agreement between persons or entities not to do business with another person or entity. In 1990, the Seventh Circuit Court of Appeals upheld the federal district court's ruling

---

7. Board of Trade of City of Chicago v. United States, 246 U.S. 231, 238 (1918).
8. "Currents: Law," *Hospitals 1990* 64, No. 9 (May 5, 1990), pp. 18, 20.

that the American Medical Association (AMA) illegally boycotted chiropractors. As part of its Principles of Medical Ethics, the AMA had passed Principle 3, which made it unethical for physicians to associate with unscientific practitioners. Chiropractors were labeled "unscientific" in a separate resolution.[9] The result was that doctors could not ethically refer patients to chiropractors, hence the illegal boycott.

If you, in concert with others, agree to sell a product or service only on the condition that the buyer also purchase a different product or service or agree not to purchase it from another supplier, you have committed a *tying* violation. For example, if you do not allow physicians to admit patients unless they agree to use the hospital laboratory, you may have committed a tying violation.[10]

However, the Supreme Court has recognized that ethical considerations and the public service nature of the medical profession distinguish the healthcare industry from other commercial activities, leading to a reluctance to apply the per se standard to the profession.[11] Consequently, alleged antitrust violations by healthcare providers should be judged under the rule of reason, rather than the more stringent per se standard.[12]

Section 2 of the Sherman Act prohibits monopolies. A *monopoly* is exclusive ownership or control of a business or business activity so as to exclude competitors. Unlike Section 1, it does not require concerted action by two or more individuals or entities. One person or a group may violate Section 2:

> Every person who shall monopolize, or attempt to monopolize, or combine or conspire with any other person or persons, to monopolize any part of the trade or commerce among the several States, or with foreign nations, shall be deemed guilty of a felony, and, on conviction thereof, shall be punished by fine not exceeding one million dollars if a corporation, or, if any other person, one hundred thousand dollars, or by imprisonment not ex-

---

9. Wilk v. American Medical Association, 895 F.2d 352 (7th Cir. 1990).
10. Thompson, pp. 5-10.
11. *See, for example,* United States v. Oregon State Medical Society, 343 U.S. 326 (1952); State of Arizona v. Maricopa County Medical Society, 457 U.S. 332 (1982).
12. *See, for example,* Virginia Academy of Clinical Psychologists v. Blue Shield of Virginia, 624 F.2d 476 (4th Cir. 1980).

ceeding three years, or by both said punishments, in the discretion of the court.[13]

To violate this section, one must have monopoly power within a market, have gotten or kept that monopoly by exclusionary or anticompetitive means, and have injured another. In other words, if you have a monopoly solely because your product is so superior or because you don't have any competitors, you have not violated the statute. However, if, for example, a physician was one of only two cardiologists in a particular market and he or she had the other's credentials suspended without cause to drive the other cardiologist out of the market, the monopoly would have resulted from exclusionary or anticompetitive means.[14] In addition, one can violate Section 2 by attempting to monopolize interstate commerce, even if the separate elements of the attempt are lawful, if the plan taken together is unlawful.[15]

The Clayton Act

Congress revised Section 2 of the Clayton Act as the Robinson-Patman Act.[16] As revised, the act regulates price discrimination by prohibiting sellers of commodities from charging discriminatory prices and purchasers from knowingly receiving favorable price discrimination. Price discrimination involves selling an identical product to different buyers at different prices that are not justified by the relative costs. It can also mean selling an identical product to different buyers at the same price without accounting for the greater cost of selling to some buyers by charging them higher prices. The act also prohibits discrimination in broker's fees, granting secret rebates, and so forth.

Section 3 of the Clayton Act invalidates exclusive dealings and tying arrangements where the effect of that conduct "may be to substantially lessen competition or tend to create a monopoly in

---

13. 15 U.S.C. § 2.
14. *See, generally,* Thompson, pp. 6-10.
15. *See* Swift & Co. v. United States, 196 U.S. 375 (1905).
16. 15 U.S.C. § 13.

any line of commerce." Sections 2 and 3 do not apply to services, only to commodities, but would apply to healthcare providers who sell commodities such as drugs.

Section 7 prohibits corporate acquisitions that tend to lessen competition substantially or tend to create a monopoly.

Section 8 prohibits a person from being a director of two or more corporations, any one of which has capital, surplus, and undivided profits aggregating more than $1 million, engaged in commerce if they are competitors, with certain exceptions such as banks and trust companies. Thus, being on the board of trustees of several competing healthcare organizations may violate the antitrust laws.[17] The act would not prevent one from being a director of both a healthcare corporation and one of its subsidiaries.

The Federal Trade Commission Act

The Federal Trade Commission Act[18] regulates conduct that is anticompetitive or of a deceptive and unfair nature. Besides making such conduct illegal, it empowers the Federal Trade Commission (FTC) to investigate possible violations and to enforce the act. The FTC has been very active in investigating and prosecuting health care providers for alleged unfair trade practices.

❖ State Antitrust Statutes

All states regulate restraints of trade, often with statutes that are similar to the Sherman Act. However, the state court decisions interpreting those laws may interpret their laws differently than the federal courts interpret the federal antitrust laws, so state laws may apply differently, or not apply, to healthcare providers.[19] Many states are more active than the federal government in enforcing the antitrust laws, and state attorneys general can bring suits not only under state law but under federal law. Thus, states try to get treble

---

17. *Id.*, pp. 11-13.
18. 15 U.S.C. § 41 *et seq.*
19. Thompson, pp. 14-17.

damages (the judge multiples the actual damages by three; see chapter 8) on behalf of the state and its citizens.

Of course both the federal and state governments have laws other than antitrust laws concerning what business practices are permissible. For example, Section 1128B(b) of the Social Security Act[20] provides criminal penalties for individuals or entities that knowingly and willfully offer, pay, solicit, or receive remuneration in order to induce business reimbursed under the Medicare or state healthcare programs. Because the prohibitions in the statute were so broad, the U.S. Department of Health and Human Services promulgated regulations setting forth proposed business and payment practices, or "safe harbors," that are not criminal offenses, effective as of July 29, 1991.[21] For example, the regulation recognizes that not all physician investments in healthcare entities to which they refer patients should be illegal by providing a safe harbor for investments in large public corporations that are available to the public.

Thus, the United States and its states have a well-developed body of law to protect free trade and commerce, expressed in the Sherman Antitrust Act, the Clayton Act, the FTC Act, and other state and federal antitrust statutes. Chapter 3 will tell you how and under what circumstances these statutes apply to the healthcare industry.

---

20. 42 U.S.C. § 1320a-7b(b).
21. Department of Health and Human Services, 42 Code of Federal Regulations Part 1001, Medicare and State Healthcare Programs: Fraud and Abuse; OIG Anti-Kickback Provisions, 56 FR 35952, July 29, 1991. *See* Jonathan P. Tomes, *The Healthcare Financial Manager's Guide to Understanding Fraud, Waste, and Abuse Issues and Safe Harbors* (Westchester, Ill.: Healthcare Financial Management Association, 1992).

Antitrust Law and the Healthcare Industry

The question of whether a particular antitrust law applies to a particular healthcare provider is complex. In general, the antitrust laws apply to healthcare professionals because health care qualifies as a profession that is engaged in interstate commerce to a degree to which the antitrust laws apply. However, you must examine the coverage of the particular statute or statutes involved. You must also determine whether your facility fits within one of the following exemptions from general coverage of antitrust laws: the nonprofit exemption, the governmental exemption, the insurance exemption, the immunity provided for peer review, or the doctrine that preempts the antitrust laws to the extent necessary to allow other laws, such as health planning laws, to operate.

❖ Does Antitrust Law Apply to Healthcare Professionals?

Before 1975, most experts believed that the antitrust laws did not apply to the learned professions, such as medicine and law. In 1975, however, the United States Supreme Court ruled that the antitrust laws did apply to members of the learned professions.[1] Consequently, one must look at the text of the antitrust statutes to see whether they cover healthcare providers, other statutes to see whether they exempt healthcare providers from an antitrust statute, and court decisions to determine whether a particular provider and its activity is covered by the antitrust laws.

❖ Application of the Antitrust Laws to Businesses and Professions

In general, the federal antitrust laws apply to all businesses and professions except the following:

- ❖ Labor unions
- ❖ Insurance companies to the extent regulated by state law
- ❖ Agricultural cooperatives
- ❖ Baseball (no logical reason for its exclusion, but it's the great American pastime)
- ❖ State action regulating the economic activity of an industry
- ❖ Lobbying and certain other petitions to influence government action, even if directed against competitors
- ❖ Certain regulated industries, but only to the extent regulated

Regulated industries, such as insurance, are only exempt from antitrust scrutiny in aspects of the business that are regulated by the states, such as the setting of rates by an insurance commission. Other aspects, such as the drafting of policy terms, are still covered under the antitrust law.[2]

---

1. Goldfarb v. Virginia State Bar Association, 421 U.S. 773 (1975).
2. *See, generally,* Matto, pp. 18-19, 157-62, and Thompson, pp. 18-20.

Antitrust law applies to all interstate commercial activity and, with limited exceptions, to both profit and nonprofit associations, partnerships, professional associations, sole proprietorships, and individuals. They apply to foreign businesses doing business in the United States and to American businesses doing business abroad. They even apply to foreign businesses doing business abroad when their activities affect American commerce, although the government may be unable to enforce them in such circumstances.[3]

Are healthcare providers involved in interstate commerce? If the facility accepts out-of-state patients, out-of-state funds and supplies, and the like, it has a sufficient impact on interstate commerce to qualify under the federal antitrust laws. In 1976, the Supreme Court ruled that because the construction of a hospital would involve purchasing supplies through interstate commerce and obtaining financing from out-of-state lenders, a conspiracy preventing the hospital's construction would have enough impact on interstate commerce to invoke the protection of the Sherman Act.[4] More recently, a federal court found that a defendant hospital's residency scheme, which subjected a certain number of residents to mandatory discharge, had sufficient impact on interstate commerce to qualify for antitrust protection.[5] Consequently, a healthcare provider who engages in strictly local purchases, sales, or services may affect commerce.

❖ The Nonprofit Exemption

Section 2 of the Clayton Act, which prohibits price discrimination in the purchase of supplies, exempts nonprofit hospitals and other charitable organizations where the institution buys the supplies for its own use. The charitable organizations language would exempt other nonprofit healthcare providers, such as HMOs. However, as a result of a 1976 Supreme Court decision, the question whether the supplies are for the facility's own use is a very complex

---

3. Matto, pp. 18-19.
4. 425 U.S. 738 (1976). *See, generally,* Thompson, pp. 15-16.
5. "Casenotes: Antitrust: Court Refuses to Dismiss Action Alleging Hospital's Pyramid Residency Program Violates Sherman Act," *Hospital Law* 32, No. 5 (May, 1990), p. 147.

one. For example, sales of drugs to former patients, to physicians who are members of the staff who dispense the medications in the course of their private practices away from the hospital, and to walk-in customers who are not patients of the hospital are not exempt. The court noted that the hospital's own use is that which promotes the facility's intended institutional operation in caring for its patients.[6]

Two other recent decisions allowed antitrust challenges to nonprofit hospitals. On August 2, 1991, the FTC reversed an administrative law judge's ruling that prohibited the FTC from challenging Adventist Health System/West's acquisition of assets from Ukiah General Hospital because both facilities were nonprofit.[7] Similarly, in FTC v. University Health Inc.,[8] the Court of Appeals for the Eleventh Circuit permitted the FTC to block University Hospital from acquiring most of the assets of another nonprofit hospital, St. Joseph's. Both of these decisions will enhance the federal government's ability to continue to aggressively challenge anticompetitive acquisitions and affiliations by healthcare providers.

Section 4 of the Federal Trade Commission Act, which prohibits unfair methods of competition and unfair or deceptive acts and practices affecting commerce, exempts nonprofit institutions from enforcement of the act.

❖ The Governmental Exemption

Hospitals that are federal, state, or local governmental institutions may also be exempt from Section 2 of the Clayton Act. In Lancaster Community Hospital v. Antelope Valley Hospital District,[9] the California local hospital district owned and operated the nonprofit defendant hospital. The U.S. Court of Appeals for the Ninth Circuit reversed the lower court's ruling, which dismissed the action because the defendant was a state entity, for two reasons:

---

6. Abbott Laboratories v. Portland Retail Druggists Association, Inc., 425 U.S. 1 (1976).
7. 1991 FTC LEXIS 354 (August 2, 1991).
8. 938 F.2d 1206 (11th Cir. 1991).
9. 923 F.2d 1378 (9th Cir. 1991).

- ❖ The state did not give the defendants the power to regulate the market, but merely allowed them to provide hospital services along with their competitors.
- ❖ The defendants violated the state's policy calling for a competitive market.

Generally, conduct of government employees that is outside the scope of the proper function of their agency is not immune from antitrust laws.

Although the exemption for nonprofit institutions that are purchasing, selling, or providing services for their own use and the exemption for governmental entities will protect many healthcare providers from liability under Section 2, many others are still liable for discriminatory purchases.[10]

❖ The Insurance Exemption

The federal antitrust laws also exempt the insurance industry to the extent that the state regulates the industry.[11] The exemption does not, however, apply to boycotts, intimidation, or coercion. Obviously, healthcare providers are involved with the healthcare insurance industry. Does this involvement fall within the exception to the antitrust laws? The United States Supreme Court decided that Blue Shield of Texas's agreements with various pharmacies to fix the retail price of drugs did not constitute part of the "business of insurance" and was not exempt from the antitrust laws. The arrangement was not part of the business of insurance because it did not involve underwriting or the spreading of risk. Rather, the agreements were merely created to purchase goods and services from participating pharmacies. Further, the agreements were not between the insurer and the insured.[12]

Union Labor Life Insurance Company v. Pireno[13] involved an insurance company's use of a peer review panel to determine

---

10. Thompson, pp. 194-99.
11. 15 U.S.C. § 1012.
12. Group Life and Health Insurance Company v. Royal Drug Company, 99 S.Ct. 1067 (1979). *See, generally,* Thompson, pp. 176-80.
13. 458 U.S. 119 (1982).

whether particular medical treatments and rates were reasonable. Because the peer review panel served only to keep the insurer's costs and, indirectly, the insured's premiums, down but played no part in the spreading and underwriting of the policyholder's risk, the insurance company was not exempt from antitrust scrutiny under the McCarran-Ferguson Act. The Supreme Court fashioned a three-part test to determine whether a particular practice was part of the "business of insurance" that was exempt under the act:

- ❖ Whether the practice has the effect of transferring or spreading a policyholder's risk
- ❖ Whether the practice is an integral part of the policy relationship between the insurer and the insured
- ❖ Whether the practice is limited to entities within the insurance industry

This decision means that many healthcare plans do not constitute the business of insurance so as to be exempt from antitrust scrutiny. These healthcare plans do not involve a risk of loss, such as the risk of having to pay a death benefit inherent in life insurance, as much as they involve quantity purchase of medical services. The plans are considered to be more like a consumer cooperative than an insurance contract.[14]

Further, the business of insurance is exempt only to the extent that state law does not regulate it. Nor does the exemption apply to boycotts, intimidation, or coercion. A *boycott* is refusal to purchase from an entity by a group acting in concert. *Intimidation* refers to discouraging another by threats, and *coercion* is pressure, such as force, that overcomes one's free will. Thus, a concerted refusal to deal with a healthcare provider by healthcare insurers could be an illegal boycott that would be outside the protection of the insurance exemption. For example, in Carl Bartholomew v. Virginia Chiropractors Association,[15] the conduct of insurers that boycotted certain chiropractors was found to be the business of insurance but could still be prosecuted as being a boycott.

---

14. *Id.*
15. 451 F. Supp. 624 (N.D. Va. 1978). *See, generally,* Thompson, pp. 182-85.

❖ Peer Review Immunity

The Health Care Quality Improvement Act of 1986[16] provides immunity for peer review actions that are taken in the "reasonable belief" that they would further quality health care and

- ❖ After a reasonable effort to get the facts
- ❖ After adequate notice and hearing procedures
- ❖ With a reasonable belief that the action was warranted

Immunity does not extend to willful and wanton actions.

In Austin v. McNamara,[17] the U.S. District Court for the Central District of California ruled that physicians who had conducted peer review investigations of a neurosurgeon and placed restrictions on his clinical privileges were immune from federal antitrust activity under the Health Care Quality Improvement Act. The central district found that the physicians acted in the reasonable belief that they were furthering quality health care, even though a review committee reversed their decision.

❖ Preemption by Other Laws

Finally, antitrust laws do not overstep the bounds of other federal and state regulatory statutes. Obviously, antitrust laws, which require free and open competition, may conflict with health planning laws, which are aimed at reducing costs through shared services. For example, in recent years the U.S. Department of Health and Human Services and Congress have through regulations and statutes encouraged hospitals to reduce excess capacity by sharing equipment and services and by consolidating. However, hospitals that have done so may thereby lessen competition, leading to antitrust scrutiny. In these situations, the federal health planning law will prevail, because the health planning law by implication repeals

---

16. 42 U.S.C. §§ 11101-11152.
17. 731 F. Supp. 934 (C.D. Calif. 1990).

the antitrust law to the minimum extent necessary to allow the health planning law to operate. The situation is more complex if a state health planning law conflicts with the federal statute. If the state itself is taking the anticompetitive activity, the state action exception discussed earlier will exempt the state from the antitrust laws. The situation is even less clear if a private provider is complying with a state planning law that conflicts with a federal statute. Certainly overt federal antitrust violations, even if arguably within state health planning regulations, may be subject to federal antitrust enforcement.[18] However, in a recent case, the court found that state immunity—the concept that the antitrust laws do not apply to state as opposed to private actions—did not protect three physician reviewers who violated antitrust laws in their peer review actions.[19]

Perhaps the increased scrutiny of healthcare antitrust issues is a logical response to the trend to eliminate or lessen competition to make the delivery of health services more efficient. One product of the tension between the goals of antitrust law and the goals of health planning is an expansion of the coverage of antitrust law to cover new arrangements by and between healthcare providers who are seeking to contain costs and operate more efficiently.

Regardless of the reason, your facility needs to determine whether it falls within or outside the exceptions of the antitrust laws before undertaking significant actions, such as a merger or the drafting of a new credentialing procedure. Obviously, you must consult your attorney. And, with the expansion of federal and state enforcement of antitrust laws in the healthcare area, a prudent approach would not include relying on an exception to the antitrust laws. Rather, your fellow officers and your counsel should seek to avoid the anticompetitive activities that violate the antitrust laws, as discussed in the following chapters.

---

18. Thompson, pp. 61-67.
19. Mary Koska, "Oregon Responds to Physician's Fears of Peer Review," *Hospitals 1990* 64, No. 1 (January 5, 1990), pp. 70-71.

Antitrust Problems in Mergers, Acquisitions, and Affiliations

Antitrust problems have arisen because many healthcare providers have had to reorganize in the past decade to increase efficiency, to eliminate duplication, and to reduce cost. This era of declining occupancy and revenues has created a need to eliminate excess bed capacity. Because of this trend, hospitals and other healthcare providers have been forced to diversify into areas other than acute care inpatient services. There has been a consolidation of hospital activities through mergers, and participation in multi-hospital networks. Freestanding institutions will likely consider cooperative relationships with third-party inpatient providers, either through management agreements, network participation, or mergers.[1]

Consolidations and affiliations can take many different forms. A facility can consolidate through a merger, an outright purchase of stock or assets of another facility, a joint venture through a pooling of assets, or the formation of a joint subsidiary. It may affiliate by forming or joining an association, a consortium, or a

---

1. Anne Murphy, "Application of Federal Antitrust Laws to Hospital Mergers: Understanding the Evolving Rules," *Hospital Law* 32, No. 4 (April 1990), p. 101 (hereinafter, Murphy).

similar organization. Even a lease or a management contract could be similar enough to an actual consolidation to receive antitrust scrutiny.[2]

If you are considering a merger or similar business reorganization, you should be aware of the increased governmental scrutiny of such arrangements for antitrust violations, understand what antitrust laws govern mergers and other such arrangements, know how to analyze a merger for antitrust problems, and know how to decrease the risk of having the government find an antitrust violation in such circumstances.

❖ Increased Antitrust Scrutiny of Mergers

Even though the federal government should want healthcare providers to meet the goals of increased efficiency and reduced cost so as to be able to provide quality health care at an affordable cost, it has stepped up its efforts to apply antitrust law to healthcare mergers, acquisitions, and other reorganizations. Congress and Health and Human Services have urged hospitals to reduce excess capacity by, among other things, consolidating where possible. However, the Justice Department has become very aggressive in protecting the public from anticompetitive collusion by rivals. Its concern is that mergers may result in a lopsided increase in market share for the merged facility compared to other facilities in the community, leading to higher prices and a reluctance to grant discounts to third-party payers. Many experts see these conflicting policies as chilling plans for mergers. For example, in early 1992, the University of Utah Hospitals and Clinics pulled out of a cooperative joint heart transplant program with three other Salt Lake City hospitals for fear of antitrust action by the Justice Department. The hospital's sensitivity to the antitrust issue stems from an antitrust investigation into two Salt Lake City hospitals for conspiring to divide up the pediatric care market in the city.[3] One commentator noted that she was "sorry to see [this] chance slip away to improve

---

2. Thompson, p. 72.
3. David Burda, "Utah University Hospital Pulls Out of Heart Transplant Cooperative," *Modern Health Care* (January 20, 1992), p. 12.

healthcare delivery through cooperation" and hoped that this "overreaction doesn't extend to other cooperative efforts that give communities an alternative to the relentless medical arms race."[4]

One study noted that 84 percent of the communities with multiple hospitals are at risk for antitrust scrutiny if any of their facilities attempt a merger.[5] In a period of declining antitrust enforcement activity in general, the Department of Justice (DOJ) and the Federal Trade Commission (FTC) have vigorously enforced the antitrust laws against healthcare mergers. In 1988, the DOJ instituted two cases to prevent proposed mergers of not-for-profit hospitals. In addition it investigated and filed administrative complaints in several other mergers.[6]

❖ Antitrust Laws Governing Mergers

As discussed in chapters 2 and 3, sections 1 and 2 of the Sherman Act, Section 7 of the Clayton Act, and Section 5 of the Federal Trade Commission Act all regulate mergers. The DOJ enforces the Sherman and Clayton Acts and can seek an injunction or damages for violations of either of them. Private parties can sue under these acts, seeking an injunction against a merger or damages caused by the merger.

However, the DOJ and the FTC evaluate the majority of mergers under Section 7 because its broad reach renders the other sections practically superfluous. Section 7 prohibits the acquisition of the stock, share capital, or assets of another entity, the effect of which may be substantially to lessen competition or tend to create a monopoly. The FTC enforces the FTC Act, which covers acquisitions through the purchase of assets as opposed to the purchase of stock. Section 5 of the FTC Act prohibits unfair methods of competition among persons, partnerships, or corporations that are in or affect

---

4. Karen Petitte, "Spooked by Antitrust Shadow," *Modern Healthcare* (February 3, 1992), p. 32.
5. Marybeth Burke, "Mixed Signals from Government Have Chilling Effect on Mergers," *Hospitals 1990* 64 (June 5, 1990), pp. 11, 36-39.
6. Murphy, p. 101.

commerce. The FTC Act does not extend to not-for-profit organizations that do not have share capital if operated for exclusively charitable purposes and not to generate profits or otherwise serve their members' business interests.

The federal government may nonetheless attempt to regulate mergers of not-for-profit entities under Section 7 of the Clayton Act. Section 7 originally applied to stock acquisitions only, but in 1950 Congress amended it to include asset acquisitions as well. However, the U.S. Court of Appeals affirmed the district court's decision in United States v. Rockford Memorial Corp.,[7] which held that courts are to read Section 7 expansively and therefore it covers not-for-profit hospital mergers that would not fall within the traditional concept of a stock acquisition by a for-profit entity. The district court characterized a merger as

- Necessarily involving the disappearance of one of the merging corporations
- Requiring shareholders of the merging corporation to surrender existing interests in exchange for new rights in the surviving corporation
- Automatically affording the surviving entity all rights, duties, liabilities, and powers of the merging corporation
- Likely resulting in continuity of management
- Giving the acquiring firm an immediate voice in the management of the corporation

Thus, according to the lower court, the consolidation of hospital corporations, as in the Rockford case, through formation of a parent corporation for the purpose of integrating hospital management and governance constitutes a merger under Section 7.[8] The Seventh Circuit did not follow this reasoning, but reached the same result by finding that although the share capital language did not apply to not-for-profit hospitals, the asset acquisition language did.

---

7. 898 F.2d 1278 (7th Cir. 1990).
8. Murphy, p. 101.

In a separate case, the Fourth Circuit, in United States v. Clarion Health Systems,[9] in an unpublished decision that has less precedent, found that Section 7 did not apply to not-for-profit hospitals. Because the United States Supreme Court declined to hear an appeal in the Rockford case, its published opinion would indicate that the prudent view (and the one being followed by the DOJ and the FTC) is that Section 7 covers mergers by both profit and not-for-profit hospitals.[10]

❖ Reporting Requirements

The Hart-Scott-Rodino Antitrust Improvement Act of 1976, as amended, requires reporting certain mergers to the FTC and the DOJ. If a transaction is valued at more than $15 million or if the purchaser would hold 50 percent or more of the voting securities of an entity with sales or assets of at least $25 million as a result of the transaction, the purchaser must report the acquisition of the voting securities or assets to the FTC and the DOJ.

After reporting the acquisition, the parties must await clearance from these agencies before consummating the transaction.[11] Filing of such a report triggers an automatic 30-day waiting period before the transaction may be consummated and may trigger a so-called second request for additional information to be supplied. Facilities considering a merger must recognize that the premerger or consolidation notification is a cumbersome, time-consuming process. A second request may result in increased costs, time lost in complying with the request, delay in consummating the merger, and the like.

If the FTC believes the merger to be improper, it may obtain an injunction to block the merger. Further, the statute contains civil penalties of $10,000 a day for failure to comply with the statute, including the reporting requirements.[12]

---

9. 707 F. Supp. 840 (W.D. Va. 1989), *affirmed*, 1989-1 Trade Cas. (CCH) ¶ 68,859 (4th Cir. November 29, 1989) (designated as unpublished).
10. *See, generally*, Murphy.
11. 15 U.S.C. § 18a.
12. 15 U.S.C. § 18a(g).

❖ Analyzing a Merger for Antitrust Problems

Once you have determined that your proposed merger or other reorganization is subject to antitrust scrutiny, you need to undertake an antitrust analysis. A financial manager will have to generate much of the financial information used to make such an analysis. An understanding of the concept of market power is important because Section 7 of the Clayton Act prohibits mergers or acquisitions that may tend to substantially lessen competition.

This is based on the theory that mergers are illegal if they create or enhance market power or facilitate the exercise of market power. Market power is the ability of one seller, acting alone, or a group of sellers, acting collusively, to hold prices above competitive levels. Thus, antitrust merger analysis must assess the effect of a merger on the existence and potential use of market power. The DOJ does this under its *Merger Guidelines*,[13] as does the FTC. These guidelines provide for a six-step process to analyze mergers, as follows:

- ❖ Define the relevant product market.
- ❖ Define the relevant geographic market.
- ❖ Calculate the market shares of the providers in the relevant product/geographic market and perform a "Herfindahl-Hirschman Index" (HHI) analysis.
- ❖ Consider other relevant factors that bear on the significance of the HHI analysis, including the factor of barriers to entry.
- ❖ Consider the existence of procompetitive or efficiency-producing effects of the merger.
- ❖ Reach a conclusion about the degree of antitrust risk of a proposed merger and assess what, if anything, you can do to decrease the risk.

In general, antitrust law, the DOJ, and the FTC determined the first element, the product market, by looking at the product in

---

13. *The Merger Guidelines of the Department of Justice*, 49 Fed. Reg. 26823 (1984), reprinted in Trade Reg. (CCH) ¶ 13,103 (1988).

question and any substitutes for that product. With regard to health care, the product market initially consisted of short-term acute care hospital services provided to doctors and patients. This market evolved first to include general acute care hospital services and later included the cluster of services offered by acute care hospitals. The cluster definition makes no distinction between inpatient acute care services and outpatient services.

The law is unclear about whether the relevant service market for hospitals includes only inpatient acute care hospitals or also outpatient services. However, a safer assumption is that hospitals considering a merger should assume that their competitors, for purposes of the antitrust laws, are other inpatient acute care hospitals. If, however, the market share evaluation shows an undue concentration, the hospital may wish to try to lay the groundwork for an argument that outpatient facilities are also competitors.[14]

A number of problems exist in determining the product market. One problem is obtaining all the information to properly make this determination. One attorney, Michael Callahan, suggests a healthcare facility obtain the following and similar information to make a record that, for example, a separate market for outpatient service exists and that additional competitors may reduce the merging entities' market share:

- ❖ The number of ambulatory surgical treatment centers, labs, free-standing or mobile magnetic resonance imagers, kidney and/or lithotripsy units, mobile cardiac catheterization units, cancer treatment centers, and other competing outpatient services
- ❖ The ability to produce these services without the need for hospital backup or the complementary services provided in the hospital
- ❖ The ability of these competing units to provide their own complementary services
- ❖ The number of physicians or physician groups providing these competing services in a freestanding or mobile unit or within their offices

---

14. Murphy, p. 101.

- ❖ A list of services that competitors can and actually do provide on an outpatient basis
- ❖ Competing clinics, independent practice associations, HMOs, and PPOs providing such services
- ❖ Home healthcare agencies
- ❖ Any studies on patient preference and other factors affecting choice
- ❖ Other competing providers of healthcare services—such as long-term care facilities, ambulance companies—and nonhealthcare services—laundry and food services, for example—that may reduce the hospital's overall market share
- ❖ Percentage of revenue generated by these competitors compared to all healthcare revenue in the appropriate geographic market
- ❖ Percentage of total revenue that the hospital's outpatient services generate compared to total revenue
- ❖ Evidence of reimbursement policies held by private and public third-party payers that promote the utilization of outpatient services
- ❖ Future trends and expansion of new product markets and competitors

Next, Callahan recommends that the facility compare the services of merging parties and notes that where the market is regional or national, the geographic market should expand to accurately reflect the source from which the facility draws 90 percent of its patients for a particular service. As the market expands, so should the number of competitors for those services, resulting in a decrease in market share. The facility should conduct market studies that its legal counsel should request (or prepare to maintain confidentiality), to determine how to accurately measure the merged parties' market concentrations by product market.[15]

---

15. Michael Callahan, "Preparing for a Hospital Merger Challenge: A Practical Approach," *Hospital Law* 23, No. 4 (April 1990), p. 115 (hereinafter, Callahan).

Defining the geographic market is no easier. Generally, the geographic market is the section of the country that would be impacted by the merger due to lessened competition. Methods of determining the geographic market include patient origin studies, the Elzinga-Hogarty Test, physician admitting patterns, and the parties' own perceptions as to their primary and secondary service areas.

The Elzinga-Hogarty Test consists of the following two measurements:

❖ A little in from outside (LIFO—not to be confused with last-in, first-out) measurement, consisting of identifying the smallest geographic area from which at least 75 percent of the larger merging hospital's patients originate.

❖ A little out from inside (LOFI) measurement that is met if at least 75 percent of the aggregate hospital business in a LIFO area is rendered to patients within that area.[16]

If more than 10 percent of patients travel into the area for hospital services or patients residing within the area travel outside the market for services, the market is too narrowly defined.

To determine the geographic market, your facility should commission studies to determine where patients go for primary, secondary, and tertiary care and consider the impact of geographic boundaries, political considerations, and other factors that may affect patient choice.[17]

The third step—calculating the market shares of the providers in the relevant product/geographic market and performing an HHI analysis—is the most significant factor in assessing the legality of a merger. The DOJ, the FTC, and the courts will likely presume an undue market share if the merged entity's market share is 30 percent or more and a significant increase in market concentration ensues. Of course, even a small share can be an antitrust violation if other factors indicate a likelihood of an anticompetitive effect.

---

16. Murphy, note 99.
17. *Id.*

The HHI quantifies market concentration by a formula that sums the squares of the individual market shares of all competing entities in the relevant market. For example, if a market contains five competing hospitals, with 30, 20, 20, 20, and 10 percent market shares, the HHI would be $30^2 + 20^2 + 20^2 + 20^2 + 10^2$ or $900 + 400 + 400 + 400 + 100 = 2,200$. The HHI must be calculated both before and after the merger. If two facilities with a 20 percent share merged the HHI would be $30^2 + 40^2 + 20^2 + 10^2 = 900 + 1,600 + 400 + 100 = 3,000$. The postmerger HHI will always be higher because it results in fewer facilities and thus higher concentrations.

The DOJ is likely to challenge mergers if the postmerger HHI is

- between 1,000 and 1,800 with a pre- to postmerger HHI increase of 100 points or more
- more than 1,800 unless the increase is less than 50 points

Thus, in our example, with a postmerger HHI of 3,000 and an increase of 800, the DOJ would most likely challenge the merger.

Note, however, that the presumption of undue market share is rebuttable. Thus, facilities intending to merge should document other factors to show that the statistical evidence does not reflect true market power or that effects favoring competition outweigh anticompetitive effects.[18]

In addition, the *Merger Guidelines* contains a list of factors, other than market share and concentration, that the DOJ will consider as to whether a presumptively illegal merger actually has an anticompetitive effect. The three that are most important with regard to healthcare mergers are barriers to market entry, weak financial condition of a merging facility, and enhanced efficiencies as a result of the transaction.

---

18. *Id.*

Barriers, which make a merger more suspect, include Certificates of Need (CON) or other federal or state restrictions on hospital construction, the high start-up costs of such construction or expansion of existing facilities, and existing excess bed capacity. Financial difficulties can help avoid antitrust liability in two ways. First, a facility must prove a grave probability that it will fail, that it cannot rectify the situation in a less anticompetitive manner, and that there is little possibility of surviving a bankruptcy reorganization. Such circumstances constitute an absolute defense, known as the "failing firm" defense. Obviously, a failed company is going to go out of the market as a competitor anyway.

Second, even if a facility is not that financially weak, i.e., it is not in danger of imminent bankruptcy, its weakness may still demonstrate, along with other evidence, a lack of an anticompetitive impact. In such a case, however, the financial weakness must be chronic, not merely the result of a temporary adverse financial climate.

Evidence of financial weakness may include the following:

- Excess capacity and deficits
- Lower profit margins
- Increase in capital cost
- Increase in competition
- Increase in Medicare/Medicaid percentage to total revenues
- Age and diversity of medical staff
- Population trends
- Continued ability to pay off long-term bonds and avoid other indicia of default
- Impact on continued delivery of quality healthcare services[19]

The third additional factor—operative efficiencies—recognizes that such efficiencies resulting from mergers will benefit consumers.

---

19. Callahan, p. 115.

Such efficiencies include economies of scale and reduced overhead. However, the merging facilities must demonstrate that no less anticompetitive means exist to achieve the efficiencies. Such efficiencies are very difficult to prove, and your facility should commission a study of projected efficiencies early in the negotiating process.[20] For efficiencies to overcome a market concentration problem, the facilities must establish by clear and convincing evidence that the efficiencies provided by the merger produce a significant economic benefit to the consumers even in light of the anticompetitive aspects of the merger. Efficiencies to consider include

- Economies of scale, avoidance of duplication, and increased specialization, complementary resources, and distribution of cost savings
- Better use of fixed cost assets
- Cost savings, taking into consideration some increased expenses
- Enhancement in quality of management and patient care
- Increase and enhancement of more sophisticated support services
- Better access to capital[21]

Finally, if the merging facilities are not-for-profit, some courts indicated that such status may reduce anticompetitive effect.[22] However, other courts have stressed that even nonprofit facilities may be motivated to act anticompetitively for the betterment of the institution even if not for the personal financial gain of its owners or shareholders.[23]

---

20. *Id.*
21. Murphy, p. 101.
22. United States v. Clarion Health Systems, *supra,* note 9.
23. United States v. Rockford Memorial Corp., *supra,* note 7. *See, generally,* Murphy, notes 153-58 and accompanying text.

❖ Decreasing the Risk of an Antitrust Violation

Now that you have considered all the foregoing factors, you can reach a conclusion about the degree of antitrust risk of the proposed merger and assess what, if anything, you can do to decrease the risk. Some techniques your facility should consider include the following:

- ❖ Obtain community support that may influence the government favorably.
- ❖ If a merger requires formal approval by the state, such as a certificate of need, argue that such approval precludes application of federal antitrust law and seek the agency's support of the merger.
- ❖ Avoid collusion to restrain trade. Any evidence of such collusion will be very harmful and the absence of such evidence, helpful.
- ❖ Develop a paper trail—records showing that the purpose of the merger was not to reduce competition, but rather its purposes were to increase efficiencies, achieve economies of scale, increase the quality of services, and so on. Your facility should also document that it cannot achieve its purposes through a less restrictive alternative.
- ❖ Document other alternatives tried, such as joint ventures, group purchasing agreements, loose affiliations with regional or national groups, and so on, and how they failed to achieve the desired goals.
- ❖ Pick a good consultant who can help the facilities realistically plan for and document all the considerations involved in the merger or consolidation. Obviously, a lawyer who is very able in the antitrust area is a must.[24]

---

24. *Id.*

Also remember the reporting requirement under the Hart-Scott-Rodino Antitrust Improvements Act of 1976, as amended,[25] discussed earlier.

Obviously, as a result of increased federal (and state) scrutiny of mergers and acquisitions and of the Rockford decision, healthcare providers who wish to increase efficiencies in this fashion must be careful to avoid antitrust liability. Although some healthcare providers appear to believe that as a result of this scrutiny and the Rockford case, they should not try to merge with another facility because of the uncertainty of the antitrust laws and the danger of legal action, the better view is that providers need not give up on such reorganizations.[26] Rather, you, as a financial manager, should help your administrators, attorneys, and consultants to provide creative arguments why the proposed action is not anticompetitive and ensure that facts and figures supporting those arguments are documented. Hospitals and other healthcare facilities have successfully merged both with and without having to litigate the antitrust aspects and will, with proper planning, continue to do so. Your facility can, too.

---

25. 15 U.S.C. § 18a (1989).
26. Daniel Higgens, "Rockford Will Not End Hospital Mergers," *Hospitals 1991* 65, No. 7 (April 5, 1991), p. 76.

Antitrust and Other Arrangements Among Healthcare Providers

Mergers and acquisitions create antitrust problems for healthcare providers, but other arrangements between healthcare providers can result in Department of Justice (DOJ) or Federal Trade Commission (FTC) scrutiny or result in a lawsuit by a plaintiff alleging harm as a result of the arrangement. For example, the U.S. Court of Appeals for the Seventh Circuit recently ruled that the American Medical Association (AMA) illegally boycotted chiropractors in violation of section 1 of the Sherman Antitrust Act. The AMA had adopted a principle that referring patients to unscientific practitioners was unethical. Another resolution labeled chiropractors as unscientific, causing them to sue.[1]

This and other similar claims are brought under two sections of the Sherman Act: Section 1, which prohibits contracts, combinations, or conspiracies in restraint of trade, or Section 2, which prohibits monopolies. If your facility is considering an arrangement

---

1. Wilk v. American Medical Association, 895 F.2d 352 (7th Cir. 1990). *See* "Casenotes: Antitrust: Federal Court Holds AMA Illegally Boycotted Chiropractors and Orders Injunctive Relief," *Hospital Law* 23, No. 12 (December 1990), p. 368.

with other healthcare providers, you need to understand how an association can violate those laws, and particular problems in this area of antitrust laws, such as the antitrust potential of HMOs and PPOs, boycotts by healthcare providers, exclusive dealing, and conversion from not-for-profit to for-profit status.

❖ Background

Ever since medieval craftsmen formed guilds, persons engaged in similar businesses or professions have joined in cooperative groups to seek solutions to common problems. However, such associations may lessen the competition between their members and lead to antitrust scrutiny.

One cannot deny the value of associations and professional societies in the healthcare field such as the American Medical Association (AMA), the American Hospital Association (AHA), and—let's not forget our publisher—the Healthcare Financial Management Association (HFMA). These associations and societies engage in beneficial activities, such as gathering and disseminating information, representing the interest of their members to the government and to the public, and standardizing or certifying the quality of the services rendered. One subset of these associations, the shared service organization, seeks to provide its members with economic advantages, such as cheaper materials though cooperative buying.[2]

❖ How Can a Professional Association Violate Antitrust Laws?

Professional healthcare associations may violate the antitrust laws by restraining trade unreasonably, such as by price fixing, or may discriminate against nonmember competitors. Thus, one way to restrain trade is to restrict membership, with its associated benefits. If hospitals will not grant privileges to those who are not

---

2. Thompson, p. 107.

members of, say, a county medical society, nonmembers cannot compete. Anyone denied membership in such an organization is a potential antitrust plaintiff, especially if membership is a requirement to practice one's profession or greatly facilitates its practice.

As far as antitrust law is concerned, the safest course is to open trade or professional association membership to all, including competitors. However, an association may establish reasonable restrictions on membership so long as the purpose of such restrictions is not anticompetitive. For example, an anticompetitive restriction would be to deny entry on the basis of membership in a competing association. Proper restrictions would be those that advance the purposes and functions of the association. Granting certification or membership privileges on the basis of skill is proper if the level of skill and the procedures for determining the level of skill are reasonable.[3]

In evaluating whether such membership limitations are reasonable, courts use the rule-of-reason test discussed in chapter 2.[4] The rule of reason requires that the judge or jury weigh "all of the circumstances of a case in deciding whether a restrictive practice should be prohibited as imposing an unreasonable restraint on competition."[5]

If the restrictive practice is to exclude a particular segment of healthcare professionals, or to prevent them from successfully practicing their profession, or if membership is an economic necessity so that without membership the nonmembers cannot compete effectively with members, the practice will not survive the rule of reason.[6] In the AMA case mentioned earlier, the court used this rule-of-reason test to find that the AMA's substantial market share coupled with the adverse effects on competition created by the boycott constituted an unreasonable restraint of trade. Of course, other arrangements, such as price fixing and boycotts, are illegal per se, and courts, the DOJ, and the FTC do not judge them by the rule-of-reason test.

---

3. *Id.*, p. 109.
4. *Id.*, p. 107-9.
5. Continental T.V. v. G.T.E. Sylvania, 433 U.S. 36, 49 (1977).
6. Thompson, p. 110.

❖ HMOs, PPOs, and the Antitrust Laws

Recently, prepaid treatment organizations, such as health maintenance organizations (HMOs) and preferred provider organizations (PPOs), have arisen as a response to the need to reduce the price of treatment without reducing quality. Such organizations have caused restraint of trade problems. In an HMO, the consumers pay a fixed fee in return for healthcare services as needed. Physicians receive a constant fee from the organization rather than reimbursement based on the cost or amount of services performed. The plan generally requires the patients to use the HMO's physicians except in emergencies.

HMOs usually take one of three forms: staff model, group, model, and individual practice association (IPA) model. In the *staff model*, the HMO employs the physicians directly. In the *group model*, the physicians are members of a partnership or corporation that enters into a contract to provide services to the HMO's subscribers. In an *IPA model*, the IPA contracts on behalf of its physician members with the HMO for the physicians to provide services to the HMO's subscribers.[7]

A PPO consists of a series of contracts among third-party payers, subscribers, and healthcare providers. Subscribers are encouraged to avoid nonparticipating physicians through certain mechanisms, for example, higher deductibles or more cumbersome methods of reimbursement. Obviously, such organizations can lessen competition.[8]

❖ Price Fixing

Any agreement that sets a maximum or minimum price may constitute price fixing. When individual competitors join together to set prices without combining other functions or creating new

---

7. Barry Furrow, Sandra Johnson, Timothy Jost, and Robert Schwartz, *Health Law, Cases, Materials, and Problems,* 2d ed. (St. Paul, Minn.: West Publishing Co., 1991), p. 472.
8. Charles Steele and Mary Huff, "Antitrust Issues Related to Health Maintenance Organizations and Preferred Provider Organizations," *Managed Health Care 1988* (New York: Practicing Law Institute, 1988), pp. 323-28 (hereinafter, Steele and Huff).

efficiencies, such a horizontal price fixing agreement is a per se violation of the antitrust laws.[9] For example, in the first criminal antitrust case the DOJ filed against healthcare providers in 50 years, it charged three dentists with violating the Sherman Act by conspiring to fix prices for dental services covered by prepaid dental plans.[10] In Arizona v. Maricopa County Medical Society et al.,[11] the U.S. Supreme Court found that Maricopa County Medical Society and another medical society that organized medical care foundations to promote fee-for-service medicine and to provide an alternative to existing health insurance plans violated section 1 of the Sherman Act. The foundations established the maximum fees the physicians could claim for health services provided to policyholders of specified insurance plans. The state of Arizona sued, contending that this arrangement was an illegal price-fixing conspiracy. On appeal, the Supreme Court held that the maximum-fee arrangements were illegal price-fixing per se violations of section 1 of the Sherman Act. In this case, the price restraint tended to provide the same economic awards to all practitioners regardless of their skill, experience, training, or willingness to employ innovative and difficult procedures in individual cases. Also, the restraint might have discouraged entry into the market and deterred experimentation and new development by individual entrepreneurs.[12]

Plaintiffs have also alleged price fixing for reimbursements by health insurance companies, contending that reimbursing only for the usual, customary, and reasonable charge constitutes price fixing. If the insurer acts alone in setting rates, its unilateral action is not prohibited by the Sherman Act. In such cases the insurer is acting as the purchaser of the services and a purchaser may determine the price it will pay. Similarly, an individual provider, acting alone, can refuse to buy goods or services or agree to work for a certain price without fear of violating the Sherman Act.

However, if a group of providers control the plan and set the rates, such may be unlawful price fixing, because those who created the HMO or PPO would be competitors but for the formation of

---

9. State of Arizona v. Maricopa County Medical Society, 457 U.S. 332, 344 (1982).
10. "Currents: Law," *Hospitals 1990* 64, No. 9 (May 5, 1990), pp. 18, 20.
11. 457 U.S. 332 (1982).
12. *Id.*, p. 348.

the new entity.[13] Thus, you should be able to avoid per se antitrust violations by avoiding provider determination of rates. However, if the insurance company sets the rates, but everyone "understands" that this is the agreed-upon price, that understanding may be sufficient to constitute a conspiracy.

Whether such an arrangement constitutes an indefensible per se violation or one that the providers can successfully defend under the rule of reason depends, in part, on the degree of integration among the providers. If providers merge completely to become an HMO or PPO, the organization becomes a single entity making pricing decisions rather than a collaborative decision by competitors, although such a merger may itself raise other antitrust problems as discussed in the preceding chapter. And, as discussed earlier, the Sherman Act does not prohibit unilateral pricing decisions. Factors such as capital contribution and sharing financial risk would demonstrate integration.

Examples of partial integration include joint marketing, centralized billing or claims processing, and collective utilization review and quality control. A partially integrated organization may be valid under the rule of reason if

- The horizontal agreements composing the venture are ancillary to a cooperative activity that promotes competition
- The collective market share of the participating ventures is not so large that it forecloses effective competition
- The parties have no anticompetitive purposes

For example, in one case, ophthalmologists joined together to offer discount eye care services. They agreed on reimbursement rates but also partially integrated their practices through pooling capital and sharing the risk of loss. Even after the arrangement, they still had a small market share and a lack of market power. The FTC found that the procompetitive benefits outweighed the anticompetitive results and did not prosecute. The FTC has stated

---

13. Steele and Huff, pp. 328-30.

that it will not take action against partially integrated plans unless either of the following applies:

- ❖ The providers formed them for anticompetitive purposes
- ❖ The plan has a substantial majority of the providers and would inhibit the development of competitive plans[14]

Thus, another way to avoid a per se violation of the antitrust rules is to at least partially integrate providers. This integration may create procompetitive efficiencies in marketing and cost containment that will avoid antitrust liability under the rule of reason.[15] If your HMO or PPO is provider-controlled, you should seek signification integration and let others—such as insulated staff (noncompetitors) or outside consultants—set prices and determine membership.

❖ Most-Favored-Nation Clauses

A *most-favored-nation clause* is a clause in a contract between a third-party payer—an insurer, an HMO, or a PPO—and a provider that requires the provider to charge the payer a fee no higher than the lowest fee the provider charges any other patient. Generally, such clauses will not violate the antitrust laws because they are the product of hard bargaining and are procompetitive. A most-favored-nation clause will have an adverse competitive impact, and be illegal, when two conditions both exist:

- ❖ The third-party payer must be so significant a factor in the market that a very high percentage of all providers feel that they must contract with it.
- ❖ The third-party payer must account for such a large portion of its providers' total billings that insufficient

---

14. *Id.*, pp. 331-32.
15. *Id.*, p. 333.

provider capacity exists to support entry into the market by other third-party payers.

Because price fixing may be a per se violation, your facility must be careful in setting prices for services or commodities.

Agreeing with competing providers to set prices can easily result in antitrust liability and expose your facility to the sanctions detailed in the next chapter.

❖ Boycotts by Healthcare Providers

As noted in chapter 2, a boycott—an agreement among a group of competitors to refuse to deal with another competitor—is a per se violation of the Sherman Act. For example, physicians in a facility could refuse to admit patients under the care of HMO physicians.[16] These agreements, often called "concerted refusals to deal," most often arise when a third-party payer will not reimburse certain providers or otherwise treats them less favorably. Such agreements also include plans to join together to prevent the creation of a health plan. As discussed in the previous section, if the third-party payer is not controlled by the providers, its refusal to deal with certain providers or anyone else does not violate the antitrust laws. However, if the payer is controlled by providers or agrees with providers to restrain trade, it will run afoul of the antitrust laws.[17]

Can an HMO or PPO refuse a provider's request to participate? Yes, but only if done for a proper reason and so long as the exclusion does not deny the provider something he must have to compete. Proper business reasons include

- ❖ Maintaining quality of care by selecting qualified providers
- ❖ Providing adequate representation of specialties
- ❖ Achieving geographic dispersion

---

16. *See, generally,* Thompson, pp. 107-31.
17. Steele and Huff, pp. 336-38.

In fact, overinclusion of providers may lead to antitrust scrutiny. If over 35 percent of providers belong to a specific PPO, for example, the Antitrust Division of the DOJ will likely scrutinize it carefully. The smaller the market share of the plan, the less likely it will violate the antitrust laws in excluding a provider.[18]

❖ Exclusive Dealing by Healthcare Providers

Another problem area is *exclusive dealing*, contractual prohibitions against participating in competing plans. If a plan has a large share of the relevant market or it inserts such prohibitions for an anticompetitive purpose, it will likely violate the antitrust laws, normally under the rule-of-reason test. However, the FTC has recognized that, in some circumstances, exclusive contracts may foster cooperative relations between health plans and providers and actually enhance competition. Certainly plans with low market shares can so contract if they do not have an anticompetitive intent or effect.

In one PPO case, the organization demonstrated how not to avoid antitrust laws when the practitioners participating in the PPO made a number of statements directed against competitors, enrolled 54 percent of the physicians in the area, and required the physicians to sign an exclusivity agreement that prevented them from contracting with any other PPO or HMO to provide medical services. Rather than give in to the DOJ's demands that it reduce its enrollment to 25 percent, abolish the exclusivity provision, and assure that it would not interfere with other healthcare delivery systems, the PPO disbanded.[19]

❖ Exclusive Contracting with Physicians

As discussed in chapter 2, a tying violation of the Sherman Act involves a concerted action requiring a buyer of a product or service

---

18. *Id.*, pp. 338-40.
19. Michael Duncheon, "Antitrust and Managed Care: A Survey of Recent Developments," *Managed Health Care 1989* (New York: Practicing Law Institute), pp. 93, 110-11.

to purchase other products or services as a condition of the purchase. Does a facility commit a tying violation by, for example, requiring every patient undergoing surgery to use the services of one firm of anesthesiologists?

The U.S. Supreme Court provided guidance concerning such arrangements in Jefferson Parish Hospital District No. 2 v. Hyde.[20] In this case, a board-certified anesthesiologist applied for admission to the medical staff of the hospital. The hospital denied his application because the hospital was party to a contract that all anesthesiological services required by the hospital patients would be performed by a professional medical corporation comprising four anesthesiologists. The doctor sued, contending that the contract was an illegal tying arrangement.

The Court reversed the lower court's ruling that the contract was illegal because the essential characteristic of an invalid tying arrangement lies in the seller's (the hospital's) exploitation of its control over the product (the operation) to force the buyer to purchase a tied product (the anesthesia services) the buyer either did not want or would prefer to purchase elsewhere. The court found the hospital did not have sufficient market power to have the requisite control over the product to constitute a tying arrangement because 70 percent of the patients in the hospital's market use other hospitals and the trial record did not contain any evidence that the hospital forced anesthesia services on any unwilling patients.

However, under this decision, a facility could commit a tying violation if it were the dominant or the only provider in a market area. Thus, before entering into an exclusive contract with a group of physicians or other healthcare professionals, your facility should have an attorney familiar with healthcare antitrust law review the arrangement.

❖ Conversions from Not-for-Profit to For-Profit Status

HMO and other healthcare provider conversions from not-for-profit to for-profit status have raised antitrust concerns. In Thomp-

---

20. 466 U.S. 2 (1984).

son v. Midwest Foundation Independent Physicians Association,[21] known as "Choicecare," a jury awarded $96 million in damages against a physician-controlled HMO and some of its officers and board members. The court found that because the physicians who controlled the HMO competed in their private practices, the setting of HMO fees constituted price fixing. Further, when Choicecare voted to write off the withholding owed to participating physicians they voted on a discount off prices and again engaged in price fixing. Before appeal, the parties settled the case, presumably for a lesser amount.[22] Associations between healthcare providers and prepaid plans are likely to increase in the 1990s and beyond. As these arrangements grow in number and size, so do the antitrust concerns of those outside the arrangements. By making certain that your facility and its personnel realize the antitrust implications of such arrangements, avoid anticompetitive intent, and enter these arrangements for procompetitive reasons, you can participate in their advantages without running afoul of the antitrust laws.

---

21. No. C-1-86-0744 (S.D. Ohio, March 14, 1988).
22. Charles Steele, "Antitrust in Managed Care," *Managed Health Care* 1989 (New York: Practicing Law Institute, 1989), pp. 163-64.

Antitrust and Access to Facilities and Organizations

Antitrust cases involving the denial or removal of privileges of practitioners for use of healthcare facilities have been in the spotlight over the last few years. One expert believes that the volume of such cases—more than in any other area of healthcare industry law[1]—results from the deep financial and psychological wounds physicians who have lost their privileges have suffered, wounds that cause them to file an antitrust suit without regard to the odds against its success and the resources required.[2]

Even though the odds against a defendant healthcare facility losing such a suit are more favorable than in other areas of antitrust law,[3] a knowledge of the principles in this area can avoid costly litigation or substantially increase the chances of prevailing in such litigation. Although a financial manager may be less involved with this area of antitrust laws than others, you can alert other key officers to the antitrust implications of hospital privileges decisions

---

1. Norbert Enders, "Federal Antitrust Issues Involved in the Denial of Medical Staff Privileges," *Loyola University of Chicago Law Journal* 17 (1986), p. 331.
2. Harold Bressler, "Antitrust Issues in the Health Care Field: An Introduction," *Hospital Law* 23, No. 4 (April 1990), p. 97.
3. Jack Bierig, "Peer Review After Patrick," *Hospital Law* 21, No. 6 (June 1988), p. 135, note 8 and accompanying text (hereinafter Bierig).

by understanding the history of regulating the practice of the healing arts, the requirement for staff privileges and peer review, their antitrust implications, and how the Health Care Quality Improvement Act's (HCQIA) limited immunity for peer review activities can immunize your facility against antitrust liability.

In addition, financial managers should be interested in this area for two reasons: ensuring that only qualified professionals practice at the facility can reduce malpractice costs and a new area of credentialing, economic credentialing, can involve financial managers.

❖ History of Regulating the Practice of the Healing Arts

Healthcare regulation has its beginnings in 1760, when the colonies created boards of medical examiners to evaluate and license individuals the examiners found qualified to practice medicine. In the mid-1800s, physicians began to form professional societies. These societies developed professional standards that the states began to use to monitor physicians. Ever since then a state license has been a prerequisite to practicing. However, most physicians need more than a state license to practice. They need hospitals and their services, particularly the high technology and support structures that hospitals alone can provide. Peer review groups decide whether to grant hospital privileges to practitioners and whether to revoke them if the practitioner fails to comply with hospital policy or procedure, provides substandard care, or engages in unprofessional conduct.[4]

❖ The Requirement for Staff Privileges and Peer Review

Healthcare facility trustees make the formal grant of hospital staff privileges to practitioners, either themselves or by adopting

---

4. Kathleen Blaner, "Physician Heal Thyself: Because the Cure, the Health Care Quality Improvement Act, May Be Worse Than the Disease," *The Catholic University Law Review* 37 (Summer 1988), pp. 1073, 1078-81.

bylaws delegating the decision-making to a committee such as a peer review group. Because many healthcare trustees are nonphysicians, they must rely heavily on staff physicians composing such peer review groups to carry out the credentialing and peer review functions to fulfill their duty of ensuring that patients receive quality medical care and are not harmed by the misconduct or incompetence of a practitioner. Although the governing board takes ultimate responsibility for failures in the quality of care its facility provides, only physicians, and often only specialists in the applicant's specialty, can undertake the technical review of the qualifications and practice required.

The Joint Commission on Accreditation of Healthcare Organizations (JCAHO) requires, as a prerequisite for hospital accreditation, that each facility establish a peer review committee as part of the hospital quality assurance program. The JCAHO standards require a single organized medical staff with overall responsibility for the quality of the professional services provided by individuals with clinical privileges, as well as the responsibility of accounting to the governing body for the quality of care.[5]

Many states have enacted statutes requiring peer committees to improve the quality of health services. These statutes generally treat the records and materials of such proceedings as privileged, so that they are not discoverable in civil proceedings or admissible in court. The statutes also immunize participants against liability for their part in the peer review process if done in good faith.[6] In addition to the state requirements for peer review, many healthcare providers have increased their peer review activities in order to ensure quality medical care to limit malpractice exposure.[7]

Many legal issues other than antitrust issues can arise from denying or revoking practitioners' staff privileges, such as confidentiality of peer review information and due process rights of applicants. However, these other issues have an impact on antitrust

---

5. Joint Commission on the Accreditation of Healthcare Organizations, *AMH Accreditation Manual for Hospitals, Standards MS.1* (Chicago: JCAHO, 1991), p. 99.
6. *See, generally,* James Hicks, "Uncertainty and Unpredictability in Application of Peer Review Privilege Statutes," *Hospital Law* 24, No. 5 (May 1991), p. 137.
7. John Graf, "Patrick v. Burget: Has the Death Knell Sounded for State Action Immunity in Peer Antitrust Suits?" *University of Pittsburgh Law Review* 51 (1990), pp. 463, 467 (hereinafter, Graf).

law. For example, the American Hospital Association conducted a survey of 3,400 hospitals that found that 58 percent of them revised the due process portions—fair hearing and appellate review—of their bylaws for fear of antitrust suits.[8] As will be discussed in detail later in this chapter, failure to afford due process can indicate that the denial of privileges was for an economic reason—to prohibit a competitor from practicing—as opposed to a proper reason, such as to ensure the quality of healthcare.

❖ Antitrust Implications of Staff Privileges and Peer Review

Obviously, getting and keeping staff privileges can create a tension between antitrust concerns and the need to ensure quality medical care. Often peer review committees comprise competitors of the practitioner under scrutiny. And the practitioner must have staff privileges for the many services only available in hospitals. Revocation or denial of privileges takes away a practitioner's ability to admit his patients to a local, convenient hospital and denies access to its expensive and sophisticated medical equipment. In addition, when a peer review committee denies or revokes a practitioner's privileges, his or her reputation is badly damaged and, because the practitioner will normally have to list such adverse decisions on staff applications, he or she will have great difficulty obtaining staff privileges elsewhere.[9]

The importance of access to these facilities has led to a modification of the rule that physicians do not have an absolute right to practice their profession in any specific hospital because patients need physicians to receive care and physicians need access to facilities to serve their patients. Thus, the courts have developed a doctrine whereby a physician has a due process right to hospital privileges if qualified.[10]

---

8. Mary Koska, "Medical Staff Changes Reflect External Pressure," *Hospitals 1990* 64, No. 22 (November 20, 1990), p. 52.
9. Graf, p. 468.
10. Paul Sciebetta, "Restructuring Hospital-Physician Relations: Patient Care Quality Depends on the Health of Hospital Peer Review," *University of Pittsburgh Law Review* 51 (Summer 1990), p. 1025, note 21 and accompanying text.

As a result of this tension between the need to police incompetent practitioners and the need to avoid anticompetitive activity, the antitrust laws in this area have developed in such a way as to either lead to or permit a lot of litigation by those harmed by such decisions without resulting in very many decisions for such plaintiffs. And such litigation has led to a reluctance on the part of practitioners to serve on reviewing boards, reluctance based on cases like Patrick v. Burget.[11]

In 1981, Doctor Patrick refused an invitation to join doctors at the Astoria Clinic and began an independent practice in competition with the clinic. As a result, he experienced difficulties with the clinic's physicians who would not refer cases to him, consult for him, or provide backup coverage for patients under his care. They then initiated and participated in peer review proceedings to terminate Patrick's privileges at the only hospital in the small town of Astoria, Oregon. The majority of the staff of the hospital were partners in the clinic. Patrick sued in federal district court, contending that the defendants had participated in the hospital peer review proceedings to reduce competition rather than to improve patient care in violation of sections 1 and 2 of the Sherman Act. The jury awarded $650,000 in damages, which the court trebled as required by the antitrust law. In addition to this approximately $2 million judgment, the court awarded $228,600 in attorney's fees.

The Court of Appeals for the Ninth Circuit reversed, finding that even if the defendants had used the peer review process to disadvantage a competitor, rather than to improve patient care, their conduct was immune from the antitrust laws because of the state action exemption. That exemption states that when anticompetitive actions are directed by a state government, they cannot be the basis of a lawsuit under the federal antitrust laws. The Ninth Circuit noted that Oregon had a policy in favor of peer review and actively supervised the peer review process.

The United States Supreme Court reversed the Ninth Circuit Court's decision, holding that the state-action doctrine did not protect the defendants from antitrust activity for their activities on the hospital's peer review committees. Part of the test for the state-

---

11. 486 U.S. 94 (1988).

action doctrine requires that state officials must have and exercise power to review such private parties' anticompetitive acts and disapprove those that are against state policy. The Supreme Court noted that the situation in the Patrick case did not satisfy that part of the test because the defendant did not demonstrate that the State Health Division, the State Board of Medical Examiners, or the courts review private decisions regarding hospital privileges to determine whether they comport with state policy or to correct abuses. As a result of the Patrick case, credentialing and peer review activities are not automatically exempt from antitrust liability absent significant state involvement in the peer review process. As a result of this case:

> Today, there are few physicians in Astoria, Oregon. Those who conducted the peer review process have been devastated emotionally and ruined financially. The case and its consequences have received enormous publicity in the medical press. And physicians across the country question whether they should serve on credentials committees or otherwise participate in peer review—lest they suffer a fate similar to the Patrick defendants.[12]

❖ The Health Care Quality Improvement Act

As a result of the verdict, Congress enacted the HCQIA.[13] Its purposes were to strengthen and encourage physician peer review activities and to restrict incompetent physicians' ability to move from state to state without disclosure or discovery of their previous incompetent performance. To accomplish this, the HCQIA

- ❖ Established a procedure for taking adverse credentialing and other disciplinary actions against physicians

---

12. Bierig, p. 105.
13. 42 U.S.C. § 11101 et seq.

❖ Provided a limited immunity for those who participate in peer review if they follow the procedure the act established

❖ Set up a National Practitioner Data Bank to receive reports of adverse professional review actions and malpractice claims, which it will report to healthcare entities who inquire[14]

To understand how this act applies to your peer review activity, you must understand the act's definitions. The hearing procedures apply to adverse professional review actions taken by a professional review body of a healthcare entity in the course of professional review activity, if the action is based on the competence or professional conduct of a physician. For purposes of the HCQIA, *physicians* includes medical and osteopathic physicians and dentists.

Under the HCQIA, a healthcare entity is a hospital or other entity that provides healthcare services and engages in professional review activity through a formal peer review process to improve health care. The entity also includes committees of the facility and professional societies, group practices, and state and federally licensed HMOs.

A professional review action is an action or recommendation of a professional review body

❖ Taken during the course of a professional review activity (a determination as to the granting, scope or condition, or change or modification of clinical privileges or membership)

❖ Based on an evaluation of the competence or professional competence of a physician

❖ Based on conduct that has had or could have an adverse effect on patient health

❖ That does or may adversely affect the clinical privileges or staff membership of a physician

---

14. 42 U.S.C. § 11134(b).

Professional review actions do not include actions based on other failings, such as failure to follow procedures regarding billing or attendance at staff meetings.

Participants in good-faith peer review activities are immune from damages with respect to conducting or participating in a professional review action that complies with the act's procedural guidelines. Likewise, persons providing information to a professional review body are immune unless they knowingly provided false information. Further, the act provides for an award of attorney's fees and costs to defendants in litigation in which the court finds that

- ❖ The defendants have met the procedural requirements of the act.
- ❖ The defendants substantially prevail in the action. This would require close to an outright, total victory for the defendant.
- ❖ The plaintiff's conduct in asserting the claim was frivolous, unreasonable, without foundation, or in bad faith.

Because the limited immunity is not available unless the professional review body follows the act's procedural standards, you should ensure that your facility's bylaws adopt them or more stringent ones. Note that the states have the option of exempting their providers from the immunity and procedural requirements of the act and some states, notably California, have done so. The procedural requirements are that professional review actions must be taken

- ❖ In the reasonable belief that the action was in furtherance of quality health care
- ❖ After a reasonable effort to get the facts of the matter
- ❖ After adequate notice of the action and hearing procedures are afforded to the involved physician or after such other procedures as are fair under the circumstances

- In the reasonable belief that the action was warranted by the facts known after the reasonable effort to get them and after meeting the notice and hearing procedures

The facility must give the physician notice, except in cases of temporary investigatory or emergency suspensions, of

- Any adverse professional review action proposed to be taken
- The reasons for the proposed action
- His or her right to request a hearing within 30 days after the notice. If the physician requests a hearing, the committee must provide him with a written notice of the date, time, and place of the hearing, and a list of the witnesses at least 30 days before the hearing.

Under the HCQIA, those conducting the hearing must be

- A mutually acceptable arbitrator
- A hearing officer appointed by the entity and not in direct economic competition with the physician involved
- A panel appointed by the entity and not in direct economic competition with the physician involved

In other words, the hearing officer or panel members should not be members of the same specialty or with clinical privileges that are substantially the same as the physician involved.

The physician facing the action has the right to

- Be represented by an attorney or other person of his choice
- Have a record of the proceedings made and a copy thereof
- Call, examine, and cross-examine witnesses
- Present relevant evidence

- Submit a written statement at the close of the hearing
- Receive a copy of the written recommendation or decision, including a statement of the basis for the decision[15]

Thus, if your facility revises its bylaws to comport with these standards or any more stringent ones required by your state, if it follows those procedures and, in good faith, takes a justified action against an incompetent or unprofessional physician, you should deter a lawsuit by that physician or, at the least, win if he does sue. And if you win, the court may award you costs and attorney's fees for defending yourself or your facility and its personnel.[16]

Also, if your state actively supervises credentialing decisions, which probably require that it, in effect, have a veto power over such decisions, your peer review activities will still be immune under the state action immunity. In addition, you can consider indemnifying members of peer review committees from liability for their participation in such activities. You should also consider affording similar protections to other healthcare professionals, such as nurses, if they are involved in peer review activities.

❖ Economic Credentialing

Recently a new twist in physician credentialing, known as *economic credentialing*, has emerged. In economic credentialing, the facility examines a practitioner's economic practice patterns as well as his or her clinical ones in determining whether to grant or continue privileges. For example, Haverford Memorial Hospital in Havre de Grace, Maryland, makes "economic efficiency of practice" a criterion for reappointment to the medical staff. To determine the economic efficiency of practice, the facility first looks at the physician's length of stay by diagnosis-related group (DRG), measured against statewide averages, and his or her charges by DRG, measured against hospital averages.

---

15. Scott Pugsley, "Implementing the Health Care Quality Improvement Act," *Hospital Law* 23, No. 2 (February 1990), p. 42.
16. *Id.*

If the physician's charges exceed 105 percent of those averages, the facility then looks at data from utilization review programs, including denials of admissions, days, and services; malpractice claims in which the physician was a codefendant with the facility in actions resulting in settlements of over $30,000; timeliness of medical record completion; and bad debts exceeding 15 percent of the total hospital charges generated by the physician. Haverford Memorial recently limited a staff physician's reappointment to a one-year term instead of the customary two-year renewal, after determining that his practice fell outside those economic parameters.

In a recent survey of more than 500 healthcare CEOs, 42 percent thought that in the next five years hospitals will consider physicians' economic contributions when renewing privileges. However, economic credentialing faces potential legal barriers such as how to develop the standards in a way that will withstand legal challenge, particularly antitrust challenge, and whether participants in peer review will lose their immunity if peer review is conducted using economic considerations.[17] In 1991, the Tennessee Supreme Court ruled that fair-hearing procedures must be followed in cases involving economic issues. The court ruled that Lewisburg Community Hospital in Tennessee erred in denying a physician access to support personnel and supplies based on economic considerations. An attorney noted that the decision rejected economic credentialing because no business-decision exemptions to the provisions of the medical staff bylaws existed.[18]

---

17. Mary Koska, "Using Profiles in the Credentialing Process," *Hospitals 1990* 64, No. 4 (February 20, 1990), pp. 34-35; and Mary Koska, "Hospital CEOs Divided on Use of Economic Credentialing," *Hospitals 1991* 65, No. 6 (March 20, 1991), pp. 42-48.
18. Linda Perry, "Tennessee Ruling Deals Blow to Economic Credentialing," *Modern Healthcare* (March 18, 1991), p. 10.

Antitrust Aspects of Pricing Healthcare Goods and Services

Price fixing of healthcare services, as discussed in chapter 5, isn't the only type of per se violation of antitrust laws. The sale of medical supplies can be a per se violation as well. Certain arrangements have a high potential for price fixing problems. To avoid antitrust liability for price fixing, you should be familiar with the Robinson-Patman Act as it applies to selling healthcare products.

❖ The Robinson-Patman Act

Congress passed another antitrust law, the Robinson-Patman Act,[1] which is part of the Clayton Act, to prevent price discrimination, improper use of brokerage fees, and discrimination in promotional and advertising allowances and services. The act makes it illegal for sellers of commodities to charge discriminatory prices and for purchasers to knowingly receive favorable price discriminations. Although hospitals and other healthcare facilities primarily

---

1. 15 U.S.C. § 13.

provide services, they also buy and sell commodities, such as drugs, other pharmaceuticals, and laboratory supplies.[2]

An entity engages in price discrimination when it does either of the following:

❖ Sells an identical product to different buyers at different prices that are not justified by the relative costs of selling to those buyers

❖ Sells an identical product to different buyers at the same price and does not account for the greater cost of selling to some buyers by charging them higher prices

Thus, an entity may sell an identical product at a different price, so long as the different price is based on the different costs of producing and selling the item to different buyers. Further, one may sell a commodity at a lower price if doing so is a good-faith response to meeting (not beating) an equally low price of a competitor. Section 2 of the Robinson-Patman Act, then, prohibits a seller from discriminating in price between different contemporaneous purchasers of commodities of like grade and quality where an anticompetitive effect is likely, unless the discrimination is cost-justified or represents a good-faith effort to meet a competitor's price. Further, Section 2(f) prohibits a buyer from knowingly receiving a discriminatory price.[3]

The Robinson-Patman Act exempts hospitals and other charitable institutions that are not operated for profit from its coverage if the facility buys the supplies for its own use. The term charitable institution covers nonprofit healthcare providers other than hospitals. As discussed in chapter 3, however, not all purchases and sales involving nonprofit healthcare providers qualify as being for their own use. In 1976, the Supreme Court broke down a nonprofit hospital's drug purchases into exempt and nonexempt categories.[4] Exempt drug sales included ones to

❖ The inpatient for use in his or her treatment in the hospital

---

2. *See, generally,* Thompson, p. 189; and Matto, p. 78.
3. Thompson, p. 191.
4. Abbott Laboratories v. Portland Retail Druggists Association, Inc., 425 U.S. 1 (1976).

- ❖ The patient admitted to the hospital's emergency facility for use in treatment
- ❖ The outpatient for personal use on the hospital premises
- ❖ The inpatient or emergency facility patient, upon discharge, and for the patient's personal use away from the hospital
- ❖ The outpatient for personal use away from the hospital
- ❖ Hospital employees or students for personal use or for the use of their dependents
- ❖ Physicians who are members of the hospital staff but are not its employees, for personal use or for the use of their dependents

The court found that nonexempt drug sales included ones to the following:

- ❖ The former patient, by means of the renewal of a prescription given when he or she was an inpatient, an emergency facility patient, or an outpatient
- ❖ Physicians on the hospital staff for dispensation in their private practice away from the hospital
- ❖ Walk-in customers who are not patients of the hospital[5]

Of course, complying with this decision can cause the facility to incur significant costs in using a dual system to account for exempt and nonexempt drugs.

Sales to the government and its agencies are also exempt from the operation of the Robinson-Patman Act. Federal facilities are completely exempt; state or municipal ones are likewise exempt in most states. However, although a cooperative association can return to its members all or any part of the net earnings on surplus resulting from its operations, they cannot engage in price fixing.

---

5. Thompson, pp. 194-95.

Thus, cooperative buyers cannot join together for the purpose of being charged discriminatory prices.[6] In this way, the Robinson-Patman Act applies to all healthcare facilities other than governmental ones and nonprofit ones to the extent that they are purchasing commodities for their own use.

---

6. *Id.,* pp. 198-99.

Sanctions for Antitrust Violations

The cost to a healthcare provider for violating the antitrust laws can be catastrophic. Among possible legal consequences your facility might face are criminal sanctions, damage awards in a civil lawsuit, an injunction against your facility, and tax consequences. Other possible consequences include bad publicity, possible loss of tax-exempt status, and the legal costs involved in avoiding antitrust litigation or defending against an antitrust claim.

❖ Criminal Sanctions for Violation of the Antitrust Laws

Sections 1 and 2 of the Sherman Act make violations of those sections a felony, punishable by a fine not exceeding $1 million if a corporation, or $100,000 if an individual, by imprisonment not exceeding three years, or both. Many states have similar penalties for violation of their antitrust statutes. The Antitrust Division of the Department of Justice in its *Sentencing Recommendations* recommends a basic sentence of 18 months for individuals and a $100,000 fine for corporations, which the judge can adjust[1] upward

---

1. Matto, pp. 138-39.

or downward depending on various factors. In 1990, the Department of Justice filed the first criminal antitrust case against a healthcare provider in 50 years and is investigating other possible antitrust violations with a view toward possible criminal prosecution.[2] The government may also file a civil enforcement suit in addition to, or instead of, a criminal indictment. The government could obtain damages or an injunction against a defendant who loses a civil enforcement action.

❖ Awards and Penalties in Civil Suits

Awards and other penalties in civil suits include damages awards, injunctions against the anticompetitive activity, tax consequences, bad publicity, and legal costs.

Damages in Civil Litigation

The real sanction in most healthcare antitrust violations is not a criminal prosecution, but a damage award in a lawsuit. If your facility commits an antitrust violation, your competitors or consumers can sue it for damages they suffered as a result of the violation. And the plaintiff may, under certain circumstances, sue on its own behalf and on behalf of all members of a group or class that was also harmed by the violation. In both cases, plaintiffs can get treble damages—three times their actual damages—plus costs and attorney's fees. Section 4 of the Clayton Act allows any person injured in his or her business or property by an antitrust violation to sue for treble damages—a powerful incentive to bring an antitrust suit. For example, in Patrick v. Burget,[3] the district court entered a treble damage judgment of $2 million plus $228,600 in attorney's fees in a case involving using peer review to eliminate a competitor. One author noted that the defendants in the Patrick case were

---

2. "Currents: Law," *Hospitals 1990* 64, No. 9 (May 5, 1990), pp. 18, 20.
3. 800 F.2d 1498 (9th Cir. 1986), reversed and remanded, 108 S.Ct. 1658 (1988).

devastated emotionally and ruined financially as a result of the judgment.[4]

In addition, defendants can be jointly and severally liable if they participated in the antitrust violation. In joint and several liability, any and all defendants are liable for all the damages and the plaintiff can decide which of them to collect from.[5]

Injunctive Relief for Antitrust Violations

An injunction is nothing more than a court order requiring the defendant against which the court entered the injunction to do or to refrain from doing something. Section 16 of the Clayton Act permits parties threatened by an antitrust violation to sue for an injunction to prevent the harm. The plaintiff need not prove actual injury; rather he must demonstrate a threat of significant harm. For example, in Wilk v. American Medical Association,[6] the U.S. Court of Appeals for the Seventh Circuit issued an injunction against the American Medical Association to stop a boycott involving the AMA's position that its members could not ethically refer patients to chiropractors. Again, the Clayton Act allows for the award of attorneys' fees and costs in suits for injunctive relief.

Tax Consequences

Section 162 of the Internal Revenue Code provides that a taxpayer may not deduct any fines paid for the violation of any law or two-thirds of any treble damage award in a civil case if convicted in a criminal case, either after trial or after pleading guilty or nocontest. Thus any criminal fine is nondeductible. Nor is two-thirds of any judgment or settlement in a civil action deductible if based on the conduct involved in a criminal antitrust case, unless it results in an acquittal.[7]

---

4. Bierig, p. 135.
5. Matto, p. 164.
6. 895 F.2d 352 (7th Cir. 1990).
7. See, generally, Matto, pp. 15-16.

Bad Publicity and Legal Costs

Considering the amount of publicity the cost of medical care receives normally, one should not be surprised that an allegation of an antitrust violation by a healthcare provider can result in a lot of adverse publicity. Terms like *monopoly* and *price fixing* sound negative when applied to the healthcare profession and its practitioners. Your facility does not need such publicity, especially the bad press a facility or its personnel would get when facing a criminal antitrust indictment. And because antitrust cases can drag on for years, the publicity can drag on for years.[8]

The legal fees involved in defending against an antitrust indictment or civil suit may also be very costly, even if the facility is exonerated of any antitrust violations. You may want to investigate the possibility of insurance for costs incurred by antitrust actions.[9]

From the foregoing, you can see that the costs of antitrust violations are substantial. However, healthcare providers can run their businesses effectively without running afoul of the antitrust laws. You can merge with another facility, or take away the privileges of a substandard practitioner, or take other business actions without violating the antitrust laws if you do it right. A knowledge of the principles of antitrust law and close coordination with other key officers and employees, particularly your attorney, can keep you out of trouble with the antitrust laws. But don't forget that the antitrust laws protect you as well as your competitors and customers. If a competitor is taking an action that violates the antitrust laws, you may sue for civil damages or an injunction to protect your healthcare facility.

---

8. *See, generally*, Matto, pp. 14-15.
9. Terese Hudson, "Ruling Highlights Hospital Antitrust Liability Concerns," *Hospitals 1991* 65, No. 4 (February 20, 1991), pp. 59-60.

Glossary

Antitrust The body of law intended to protect trade and commerce from unlawful restraints and monopolies.

Boycott The act of refusing to deal with an entity.

CEO An acronym for Chief Executive Officer. The officer responsible for running the day-to-day activities of a business.

Certificate of Need A document issued by a state as a prerequisite to opening or expanding a healthcare facility.

Clayton Act A federal law that supplements the Sherman Act's prohibitions against unlawful restraints and monopolies.

Credentialing The act of approving a healthcare professional's access to healthcare facilities. The granting of hospital or other related privileges.

Department of Justice The federal agency responsible for prosecuting criminal and civil actions on behalf of the federal government. Its Antitrust Division, along with the Federal Trade Commission, enforces the antitrust laws.

Elzinga-Hogarty Test A method of determining a healthcare provider's geographic market to determine whether a merger violates antitrust laws.

Exclusive Dealing A contractual prohibition against dealing with those who are not a party to the contract.

Federal Trade Commission The federal agency responsible for enforcing the antitrust laws.

Federal Trade Commission Act The statute creating the Federal Trade Commission and making unfair methods of competition and unfair or deceptive acts or practices in or affecting commerce unlawful.

Geographic Market The section of the country in which the effects of a merger would be felt.

Group Boycott An agreement between persons or entities not to do business with another person or entity.

Hart-Scott-Rodino Antitrust Improvements Act A federal statute that requires parties considering a merger to report information to the federal government.

HCQIA Acronym for the Health Care Quality Improvement Act.

Health Care Quality Improvement Act A federal statute that establishes procedures for peer review, provides limited immunity for those who participate therein, and sets up a data bank to collect information on substandard practitioners.

Health Maintenance Organization A healthcare entity in which the consumers pay a fixed fee in return for healthcare services.

Herfindahl-Hirschman Index A test used to analyze mergers that quantifies market concentration by a formula that sums the squares of all competing entities in the relevant market.

HHI Acronym for Herfindahl-Hirschman Index.

HMO Acronym for Health Maintenance Organization.

Hospital Governing Board The group that sets the policy of the institution.

Immunity An exemption from the operation of a law.

Injunction A court order directing someone to do or to refrain from doing an action.

Insurance Exemption The doctrine that exempts insurance providers to the extent that state law regulates them.

Interstate Commerce Commercial activities between citizens and inhabitants of different states.

JCAHO Joint Commission on the Accreditation of Healthcare Organizations.

Joint Venture A business undertaking by two or more entities under which they share the profits, loss, risk, and control. Usually involves a shorter period than a partnership.

Limited Immunity A less-than-total exemption from the coverage of a statute, usually requiring the party seeking immunity to have acted in good faith.

Market Power The ability of one seller, or a group of sellers acting collusively, to hold prices above competitive levels.

Merger A consolidation of corporations in which only one of two or more survives or that brings a new corporation into being, ending the existence of the former ones.

Monopoly The absolute control, by one entity, of the purchase, sale, manufacture, or use of a particular good or service.

Most-Favored-Nation Clause A contract clause that requires the provider to charge the payer of health services bills a fee no higher than the lowest fee the provider charges any other patient.

Nonprofit Exemption The concept that exempts hospitals and other nonprofit entities from certain of the antitrust laws.

Peer Review The scrutiny of healthcare professionals by those with similar credentials to determine whether they should have access to health facilities.

Per Se Rule The more severe of the two tests used to determine whether a particular action violates the antitrust rules. Under this test, the action is always illegal regardless of the circumstances.

PPO Acronym for Preferred Provider Organization.

Preemption A legal doctrine that makes inferior, such as state, laws inoperative to the extent they conflict with superior, most often federal, ones.

Preferred Provider Organization A series of contracts between third-party payers, subscribers, and healthcare providers in which subscribers are encouraged to avoid nonparticipating providers.

Price Discrimination Charging different prices to different customers for reasons that do not take into account differences in cost of manufacture, transportation, or sale.

Price Fixing The unlawful setting of prices by competitors.

Robinson-Patman Act A portion of the Clayton Act that prohibits price discrimination involving commodities.

Rule of Reason The less severe of the two tests used to determine whether a particular action violates the antitrust laws. Unlike the per se rule, the court will look at the circumstances to determine whether a violation exists.

Sherman Act A federal law to protect trade and commerce from unlawful restraints and monopolies.

Treble Damages An award in an antitrust case consisting of three times the amount of a plaintiff's actual damages.

Trustee One who holds a fiduciary position of trust and confidence to oversee an organization.

Tying Violation An agreement to buy or sell a product or service only on the condition that the buyer or seller agrees not to deal with any others or must buy other products or services from the seller.

Bibliography

American Medical Association. *A Compendium of State Peer Review Immunity Laws.* Chicago: The American Medical Association, 1988.

Anderson, Howard. "Legal and Strategic Consulting Most in Demand." *Hospitals 1990* 64, No. 13 (July 5, 1990), pp. 22-27.

Berman, Howard, Lewis Weeks, and Steven Kukla. *The Financial Management of Hospitals,* 7th ed. Ann Arbor, Mich.: Health Administration Press, 1990.

Bierig, Jack. "Peer Review After Patrick." *Hospital Law* 21, No. 6 (June 1988), p. 135.

Blaner, Kathleen. "Physician Heal Thyself: Because the Cure, the Health Care Quality Improvement Act, May Be Worse Than the Disease." *The Catholic University Law Review* 37 (Summer 1988), pp. 1073, 1078-81.

Bressler, Harold. "Antitrust Issues in the Healthcare Field: An Introduction," *Hospital Law* 23, No. 4 (April 1990), p. 101.

Burda, David. "Utah University Hospital Pulls Out of Heart Transplant Cooperative." *Modern Health Care* (January 20, 1992), p. 12.

Burke, Marybeth. "Mixed Signals from Government Have Chilling Effect on Mergers." *Hospitals 1990* 64 (June 5, 1990), pp. 11, 36-39.

Callahan, Michael. "Preparing for a Hospital Merger Challenge: A Practical Approach." *Hospital Law* 23, No. 4 (April 1990), p. 115.

Caruana, Russell. *Organizing a Healthcare Financial Services Division*, 3d ed. Westchester, Ill.: Healthcare Financial Management Association, 1990.

Duncheon, Michael. "Antitrust and Managed Care: A Survey of Recent Developments." *Managed Health Care 1989*, pp. 93, 110-11. New York: Practicing Law Institute, 1989.

Enders, Norbert. "Federal Antitrust Issues Involved in the Denial of Medical Staff Privileges." *Loyola University of Chicago Law Journal* 17 (1986), p. 331.

Furrow, Barry, Sandra Johnson, Timothy Jost, and Robert Schwartz. *Health Law, Cases, Materials, and Problems*, 2d ed. St. Paul, Minn.: West Publishing Co., 1991.

Graf, John. "Patrick v. Burget: Has the Death Knell Sounded for State Action Immunity in Peer Antitrust Suits?" *University of Pittsburgh Law Review* 51 (1990), pp. 463, 467.

Hicks, James. "Uncertainty and Unpredictability in Application of Peer Review Privilege Statutes." *Hospital Law* 24, No. 5 (May 1991), p. 137.

Higgens, Daniel. "Rockford Will Not End Hospital Mergers." *Hospitals 1991* 65, No. 7 (April 5, 1991), p. 76.

Holmes, William. *1990 Antitrust Handbook*. New York: Clark Boardman Co., Ltd., 1990.

Hudson, Terese. "Ruling Highlights Hospital Antitrust Liability Concerns." *Hospitals 1991* 65, No. 4 (February 20, 1991), pp. 59-60.

Joint Commission on the Accreditation of Healthcare Organizations. *Accreditation Manual for Hospitals, 1992 Standards*. Chicago: JCAHO, 1992.

Koska, Mary. "Oregon Responds to Physician's Fears of Peer Review." *Hospitals 1990* 64, No. 1 (January 5, 1990), pp. 70-71.

Koska, Mary. "Using Profiles in the Credentialing Process." *Hospitals 1990* 64, No. 4 (February 20, 1990), pp. 34-35.

Koska, Mary. "Medical Staff Changes Reflect External Pressure." *Hospitals 1990* 64, No. 22 (November 20, 1990), p. 54.

Koska, Mary. "Hospital CEOs Divided on Use of Economic Credentialing." *Hospitals 1991* 65, No. 6 (March 20, 1991), pp. 42-48.

Letwin, William. *Law and Economic Policy in America.* 1965.
Matto, Edward. *A Manager's Guide to the Antitrust Laws.* New York: AMACOM, 1980.
Murphy, Anne. "Application of Federal Antitrust Laws to Hospital Mergers: Understanding the Evolving Rules." *Hospital Law* 32, No. 4 (April 1990), p. 101.
Perry, Linda. "Tennessee Ruling Deals Blow to Economic Credentialing." *Modern Healthcare* (March 18, 1991), p. 10.
Petitte, Karen. "Spooked by Antitrust Shadow." *Modern Healthcare* (February 3, 1992), p. 32.
Pugsley, Scott. "Implementing the Health Care Quality Improvement Act." *Hospital Law* 23, No. 2 (February 1990), p. 42.
Sciebetta, Paul. "Restructuring Hospital-Physician Relations: Patient Care Quality Depends on the Health of Hospital Peer Review." *University of Pittsburgh Law Review* 51 (Summer 1990), p. 1025.
Steele, Charles, and Mary Huff. "Antitrust Issues Related to Health Maintenance Organizations and Preferred Provider Organizations." *Managed Health Care 1988*, pp. 323-28. New York: Practicing Law Institute, 1988.
Thompson, Martin V. *Antitrust and the Healthcare Provider.* Germantown, Md.: Aspen Systems Corp., 1979.
Tomes, Jonathan P. *The Healthcare Financial Manager's Guide to Fraud, Waste, and Abuse Issues and Safe Harbors.* Westchester, Ill.: Healthcare Financial Management Association, 1992.
Tomes, Jonathan P. *The Trustee's Guide to Peer Review and Credentialing.* Westchester, Ill.: Healthcare Financial Management Association, 1992.
Unland, James J. *The Trustee's Guide to Understanding Hospital Business Fundamentals.* Westchester, Ill.: Healthcare Financial Management Association, 1991.
U.S. Department of Health and Human Services, Public Health Service, Health Resources and Services Administration, National Practitioner Bank. *A Reference for Individuals and Entities Reporting to and Querying the Data Bank.* Washington, D.C.: U.S. Department of Health and Human Services, 1990.

Index

A
Abbott Laboratories v. Portland Retail Druggists Association, Inc., 16, 60
Access to capital, 32
Acquisitions, 2–3, 21–35
 Clayton Act prohibit of anticompetitive, 11
Affiliations, 2–3, 21–34
Antitrust law
 access to facilities and organizations under, 47–57
 applications to businesses and professions of, 14–15
 history and background of, 5–6
 overview of, 5–12
 per se violation of, 8, 39, 41, 59
 preemption of, 19–20
 professional organization violations of, 35–45
 sanctions, 63–66
Antitrust problems, 1–2, 21–34
 decreasing the risk of, 33–34
Associations, professional, 35
 evolution of, 48
 increased growth projected for, 45
 restrictions on membership in, 37
 violations of antitrust laws by, 36–37
Attorney's representation, 55
Austin v. McNamara, 19
Avoidance of duplication, 32

B
Bibliography, 71–73
Board of Trade of City of Chicago v. United States, 8
Boycott
 defined, 18, 42
 group, 8–9
 by healthcare providers, 42–43
 illegal, 37
Bylaws, incorporation of HCQIA's procedural standards to facility's, 54, 56

C
Callahan, Michael, 27–28
Carl Bartholomew v. Virginia Chiropractors Association, 18
Certificates of Need (CON), 31
Civil suits for antitrust violations
 bad publicity resulting from, 66
 damages in, 64–65
 injunctive relief in, 65
 legal costs of, 66
 tax consequences of damages paid in, 65
Clayton Act, 5
 Robinson-Patman Act as previous Section 2 of, 10, 5
 Section 2 prohibition of price discrimination, 15–17
 Section 3 invalidation of tying arrangements, 10–11
 Section 7 prohibition of corporate acquisitions that reduce competition, 11, 23–26
 Section 8 prohibition of directorships in competing organizations, 11
Coercion defined, 18
Collusion to restrain trade, 33
Community support of proposed merger, 33
Competition
 antitrust legislation to address lessening of, 20, 26
 enhanced by some exclusive contracts, 43
 HMO and PPO potential to lessen, 38
 market analysis for, 27–28
 by nonmembers of professional associations, 36–37
 peer review used to lessen, 51–52

Consultants
 facilities planning, 33
 legal, 1
Continental T.V. v. G.T.E. Sylvania, 37
Conversion from not-for-profit to for-profit status by providers, 44–45
Cooperative associations for purchasing, 61–62
Cost savings, 32

D

Department of Health and Human Services, U.S., 12, 19
 excess hospital capacity studied by, 22
Department of Justice (DOJ), U.S., 22–23
 challenges to mergers by, 30, 35
 reporting requirements to, 25
 sanction recommendations by, 63–64
Diagnosis-related group (DRG) length of stay averages, 56–57
Division of markets defined, 8
Documentation of proposed mergers, 33
Drugs, sales of, 16
Due process requirements for applicants for staff privileges, 49–50

E

Economic credentialing, 56–57
Economies of scale, 32
Elzinga-Hogarty test, 29
Enhanced efficiencies from mergers, 30–32
Exclusive contracting with physicians, 43–44
Exclusive dealing by healthcare providers, 43

F

Federal Trade Commission (FTC)
 enforcement of antitrust laws against healthcare mergers, 23, 40–41
 investigative powers of, 11, 16
 Merger Guidelines of, 26, 30
 mergers scrutinized by, 35
 reporting requirements to, 25
Federal Trade Commission Act, 5, 11
 Section 4 prohibition of unfair competition, 16
 Section 5 regulation of mergers, 23–24
Financial condition of merging facility, 30–31
Fixed cost assets, 32
FTC v. University Health Inc., 16

G

Geographic market, 28–29
Glossary, 67–70
Goldfarb v. Virginia State Bar Association, 14
Government
 civil suits filed by, 64
 medical product sales to, 61–62
Governmental exemption from Section 2 of Clayton Act, 16–17
Group boycott defined, 8–9
Group Life and Health Insurance Company v. Royal Drug Company, 17
Group model of HMO, 38

H

Hart-Scott-Rodino Antitrust Improvement Act of 1976, 25, 34
Haverford Memorial Hospital, 56–57
Health Care Quality Improvement Act (HCQIA) of 1986, 19
 defendants' rights under, 54
 hearings under, 55

immunity for peer review activities under, 48, 53–54
physicians' rights under, 55–56
professional review action under, 53–55
restrictions on incompetent physicians under, 52
Health maintenance organizations (HMOs)
antitrust potential of, 36, 38
conversion from not-for-profit to for-profit status by, 44–45
models of, 38, 41
refusal for provider's participation in, 42–43
restraint of trade problems with, 38–40
Healthcare antitrust, 13–20
goods and services by providers under, 59–62
potential for, 3
problem, 1–3
staff privileges and professional memberships under, 47–57
Healthcare providers
arrangements among, 35–45
bylaws for, antitrust protection in, 54–55
conversion to for-profit status by, 44–45
exclusive dealing by, 43
history of regulation of, 48
Herfindahl-Hirschman Index (HHI) analysis, 26, 29–30

I

Individual practice association (IPA) model, 38
Insurance company reimbursements, price fixing in, 39
Insurance exemption from antitrust laws, 17–18
Internal Revenue Code, tax consequences of paying damages under, 65
Interstate Commerce Act, 6

Interstate Commerce Commission, 6
Intimidation defined, 18

J

Jefferson Parish Hospital District No. 2 v. Hyde, 44
Joint Commission on Accreditation of Healthcare Organizations (JCAHO) requirements for accreditation, 49
Joint subsidiary, 21
Joint ventures, consolidation through, 21

L

Labor Life Insurance Company v. Pireno, 17–18
Lancaster Community Hospital v. Antelope Valley Hospital District, 16–17
Legal fees from antitrust indictment or civil suit, 66
Little in from outside (LIFO) measurement, 29
Little out from inside (LOFI) measurement, 29

M

McCarran-Ferguson Act, 18
Market entry, barriers to, 30–31
Market share
calculating, 29–30
collective, size of, 40
evaluation, 27
Market studies, 28
Mergers, 2–3, 21–35
analysis for antitrust problems of, 26–32
decreasing risk of antitrust violations for, 33–34
documenting, 33
reporting requirements for, 25
Monopolies
defined, 9
prohibited by Sherman Antitrust Act, 7, 9–10

Most-favored-nation clauses, conditions for adverse competitive impact in, 41–42

N
National Practitioner Data Bank to store adverse professional review actions, 53

P
Partial integration of providers, 40
Patrick v. Burget, 49, 51–52, 64–65
Peer review
  actions, immunity for physicians conducting, 19, 48
  antitrust implications for, 50–52
  confidentiality issues of, 49
  requirement for, 48–50
Peer review committee, JCAHO requirement for, 49
Per se rule, 8–9
Physician admitting patterns, 29
Physicians
  damage from loss of privileges to, 47, 50
  notice of professional review actions to, 55
  rights during professional review actions of, 55–56
Preferred provider organizations (PPOs), 41
  antitrust potential of, 36
  refusal for provider's participation in, 42–43
  restraint of trade problems with, 38–40
Price discrimination defined, 10
Price fixing, 36–41, 59–62
  bad publicity to providers from, 66
  defined, 8, 38
  by health insurance companies, 39
  horizontal, 29
Pricing healthcare goods and services, antitrust law and, 59–62

Principles of Medical Ethics, 9
Product market, 26–29
Product sales
  exempt and nonexempt categories for, 60–61
  to the government, 61–62
  price discrimination in medical, 59–62
Professional review actions
  awards under, 54
  decision of, 56
  evidence at, 55
  notice to physicians under, 55
  officers conducting, 55
  physicians' rights during, 55–56
  procedural requirements for, 54–55
  recording of, 55
  witnesses at, 55
Public hospitals, anticompetitive activity at, 2
Purchasing, discrimination in, 59–62

R
Restraint of trade. *See also* Price fixing
  collusion in, 33
  by HMOS and PPOs, 38–40
  laws to prevent, 7, 23, 35
  by professional associations, 36
Robinson-Patman Act, 10, 59–62
  Section 2 prohibition of price discrimination, 60
Rule-of-reason test, 7–8, 37

S
Sanctions for antitrust violations, 63–66
  under the Clayton Act, Section 4, 64
  under the Clayton Act, Section 16, 65
  under the Sherman Act, Sections 1 and 2, 63–64
Service market, 27

Sherman Antitrust Act (1890), 5–10
  per se violation of, 8, 42
  sanctions under, 63–64
  Section 1 prohibition of restraint of trade, 7, 23, 35, 39, 51
  Section 2 coverage of monopolies, 7, 9–10, 23, 35, 51
  tying violations of, 9, 43–44
Social Security Act, Section 1128B(b) criminal penalties, 12
Societies of professionals. *See* Associations, professional
Staff model of HMO, 38
Staff privileges
  antitrust implications for, 50–52
  antitrust law and, 47–57
  due process rights of applicants for, 49–50
  economic credentialing in, 56–57
  requirement for, 48–50
State antitrust statutes, 5, 11–12
State of Arizona v. Maricopa County Medical Society, 9, 39
State statutes requiring peer committees, 49
States' rights to exempt providers from HCQIA peer reviewer immunity, 54

Support services, increase and enhancement of, 32
Swift & Co. v. United States, 10

T
Thompson v. Midwest Foundation Independent Physicians Association, 44–45
Tying violation, 9, 43–44

U
United States v. Clarion Health Systems, 25, 32
United States v. Oregon State Medical Society, 9
United States v. Rockford Memorial Corp., 24, 32, 34
United States v. Topco Associates Inc., 6
Utilization review programs, 57

V
Virginia Academy of Clinical Psychologists v. Blue Shield of Virginia, 9

W
Wilk v. American Medical Association, 9, 35, 37, 65

About the Author

Jonathan P. Tomes is an associate professor at IIT Chicago-Kent College of Law. Among the subjects he has taught is administrative law—the part of the law that deals with the rules and regulations that administrative agencies, such as the Environmental Protection Agency, Health and Human Services, the Occupational Safety and Health Administration, and so forth, issue to control publicly regulated businesses such as healthcare providers and hospital law.

Before going to law school, Professor Tomes served as an infantry platoon leader in Vietnam, where he won the Silver Star and the Combat Infantry Badge among other awards. Then he graduated first in his class at Oklahoma City University School of Law and won the Oklahoma Bar Association outstanding law student award. He is a member of the Illinois and Oklahoma bars. Following graduation, he served in the Judge Advocate General's Corps, U.S. Army, until he retired as a lieutenant colonel in 1988. While in the military, he served as prosecutor, defense counsel, and military judge before becoming Chief of Special Claims, Tort Claims Division, U.S. Army Claims Service, where he was in charge of processing and adjudicating claims that occurred overseas against the military, primarily medical malpractice claims. That assignment led to his interest in healthcare law. The military rewarded his twenty years' service by awarding him the Legion of Merit, the second-highest service award in the military, upon his retirement.

Among Professor Tomes's publications are *The Servicemember's Legal Guide*, *Healthcare Records: A Practical Legal Guide*, *The Trustee's Guide to Understanding Healthcare Environmental Law*, *The*

Trustee's Guide to Understanding Healthcare Antitrust Law, The Trustee's Guide to Understanding Peer Review and Credentialling, and articles in the *Boston University Annual Review of Banking Law, Richmond Law Review, Air Force Law Review* (the U.S. Supreme Court cited his article in this law review), and *The Practical Lawyer.*